EDITOR
WILLIS F. OVERTON
Temple University

EDITORIAL ASSISTANT
DANIELLE L. HORVATH
Temple University

MONOGRAPHS OF THE SOCIETY FOR RESEARCH IN CHILD DEVELOPMENT

Serial No. 264, Vol. 66, No. 1, 2001

CONTENTS

COMMENTARY

ABSTRACT

ANDERSON, DANIEL R.; HUSTON, ALETHA C.; SCHMITT, KELLY; LINEBARGER, DEBORAH L.; and WRIGHT, JOHN C. Early Childhood Television Viewing and Adolescent Behavior: The Recontact Study. *Monographs of the Society for Research in Child Development*, 2001, **66**(1, Serial No. 264).

In this *Monograph*, we report the follow-up of 570 adolescents who had been studied as preschoolers in one of two separate investigations of television use. The primary goal of the study was to determine the long-term relations between preschool television viewing and adolescent achievement, behavior, and attitudes. Using a telephone interview and high school transcripts, we assessed adolescent media use; grades in English, science, and math; leisure reading; creativity; aggression; participation in extracurricular activities; use of alcohol and cigarettes; and self-image. In each domain, we tested theories emphasizing the causal role of television content (e.g., social learning, information processing) as contrasted with those theories positing effects of television as a medium, irrespective of content (e.g., time displacement, pacing, interference with language).

The results provided much stronger support for content-based hypotheses than for theories emphasizing television as a medium; moreover, the patterns differed for boys and girls. Viewing educational programs as preschoolers was associated with higher grades, reading more books, placing more value on achievement, greater creativity, and less aggression. These associations were more consistent for boys than for girls. By contrast, the girls who were more frequent preschool viewers of violent programs had lower grades than those who were infrequent viewers. These associations held true after taking into account family background, other categories of preschool viewing, and adolescent media use. One hypothesis accounting for the sex differences is that early experiences, such as television viewing, have greater effects when they counteract normative developmental trends and predominant sex-typed socialization influences than when they reinforce them.

Adolescents in the study used both television and print media to support ongoing interests. Television content (e.g., entertainment, sports, or world events) predicted extracurricular activities, role models, and body image. The only evidence for possible effects of television as a medium was the positive relation of total viewing to obesity for girls.

The medium of television is not homogeneous or monolithic, and content viewed is more important than raw amount. The medium is *not* the message: The message is.

I. INTRODUCTION

Historically, each new medium of mass communication has, within a few years of its introduction, been condemned as a threat to the young people who use it most. Typically the new medium has been blamed for capturing excessive time and interest of children and youth, for corrupting their values, for wasting time that would otherwise have been spent more constructively, and for causing a decline in taste, morality, self-discipline, learning, and socialization. Whether the new medium has been paperback books, telephones, comic books, movies, radio, television, video games, or the World Wide Web, it has been assumed to have homogeneous use and content. It has therefore been held responsible for captivating the younger generation with a level of passive engagement that was close to addiction and for generating an indiscriminate fascination with all its messages regardless of their content, validity, merit, or relevance to the life of the child. On the heels of fears about the medium itself have come concerns about content that will corrupt moral values and stimulate undesirable behavior. In the United States, we vacillate between alarms about violence and concerns about sex on the media, with each new medium raising alarm that it poses greater threats than those that preceded it.

At the same time, new media have been greeted with optimism about their potential for expanding the horizons of the young and for offering powerful new tools for teaching and learning. With respect to television, the focus of this *Monograph*, educators and others saw its potential for providing information in an interesting and engaging form. By the end of the 1960s, two pioneering educational programs for young children, *Sesame Street* and *Mister Rogers' Neighborhood,* had established the power of broadcast television for informing and educating young children.

1

GOALS OF THE STUDY

In this *Monograph*, we examine the associations between television viewing in early childhood and adolescent characteristics that are most often alleged to be initiated, determined, or enhanced by exposure to television, including academic achievement, creativity, reading, involvement in extracurricular activities, self-image, identification with role models, health behaviors, and aggressiveness. We were guided by a rich set of theoretical hypotheses in both the scientific and popular literatures on television and children, many of which are mutually contradictory. We believe the results of our research help reduce the different (and often passionately held) beliefs to a few empirically supported and mutually consistent hypotheses that we hope can be used to articulate a scientifically defensible set of public policies about media for children and can form the nucleus of a research agenda for further understanding this important part of the ecology of childhood.

THEORIES ABOUT MEDIA AND CHILDREN'S DEVELOPMENT

Theories about the roles of television in the lives of children and adolescents fall into two broad classes: those that emphasize the content presented and those that focus on amount of exposure to the medium irrespective of its content. Within each of these broad categories, some theories propose "effects" of television on viewers; others stress the viewer's active role in selecting and using media for particular purposes.

Content-Based Theories About Television Effects

If television's impact is due primarily to its content, and if the content of television is not uniform, then the impact of television varies according to viewers' patterns of exposure to different types of programs. In general, content-based theories predict that programs providing educational messages and displaying models of appropriate behavior should have a positive impact on those who view them and that exposure to inappropriate, misleading, and antisocial messages should have a negative impact.

Learning and Information Processing

Observational learning theory (e.g., Bandura, 1994) and information processing theories (e.g., Huesmann, 1986) are both designed to explicate

the mechanisms by which people learn social information froı.
but they can be applied to all types of content. In their broaɑ
these theories lead to the prediction that children attend to, encoᴜ
store in memory the information and behavior they see and hear on
vision or in other media and that they use that information to guı,
their own interests, motivations, and actions. According to Bandura (1994),
processes of attention and retention are the core of learning from viewing. Once information is stored in memory, it can endure even in the
absence of any behavioral manifestation until environmental cues or individual motivational processes lead to its expression. Repeated rehearsal,
including covert or mental rehearsal of images, is likely to strengthen
them and make them more available for activation at a later time. People
who are attractive, warm and nurturing, powerful, and/or similar to the
observer are most likely to draw attention, become role models, and be
emulated (Bandura, 1977).

Huesmann (1986; Huesmann & Miller, 1994) proposed that television content contributes to children's cognitive scripts: learned patterns
of action that lead to expectations about others, one's own behavior, consequences of that behavior, and acceptable forms of social problem solving. Repeated viewing leads children to retrieve, rehearse, solidify, and
expand existing scripts, resulting in cumulative long-term effects. Children who identify with media characters and who consider television a
realistic reflection of the world are especially likely to incorporate and
act on its messages.

Although both of these theories were originally developed to understand media effects on social behavior, the same principles can be applied to cognitive and academic content. These principles lead to the
"early learning hypothesis": that children learn a wide range of content
from television, including letters, numbers, concepts, vocabulary, and creativity. Moreover, academic achievement may be affected indirectly by exposure to violent content because aggressive behavior tendencies interfere
with learning, especially in school (Huesmann & Eron, 1986).

Cultivation

Cultivation theorists reject the language of television "effects" and instead propose an incremental process by which television messages become incorporated in viewers' conceptions of the real world (Signorielli
& Morgan, 1990). Because there are common messages in much of the
available programming, cultivation theorists argue that exposure to any
television is likely to instantiate the same beliefs. We take exception to
the assumption that all television has common messages, but content analyses do show that there are pervasive messages in the bulk of commercial

entertainment programming, for example, that glamour, strength, and physical attractiveness are paramount and that success can be obtained with relatively little work (Signorielli & Morgan, 1990).

Content Theories Emphasizing Active Viewers

Both developmental psychologists and communications theorists have argued that people of all ages use media actively to fulfill many functions, choosing both medium and content to suit particular motives, interests, and abilities. Such a view does not negate the importance of content or of the medium itself but requires an analysis that takes into account the characteristics of individuals in conjunction with the characteristics of the medium. A child or adolescent may select a variety of media depending on whether the immediate need is for information, entertainment, relaxation, or background noise (Rosengren, Wenner, & Palmgreen, 1985). In this framework, television might facilitate or inhibit interest in other activities. For example, children may have different levels of interest in *Sesame Street*, leading to different amounts of viewing. Among adolescents, viewing television programs about sports and reading the sports page in the newspaper could both activate and result from active participation in sports. When people view television, they may learn its content, and that experience may lead to changes in later patterns of attention and interest. The direction of causation is both from individual to media choice and from media content to learning, with the interchange continuing over time.

Effects of the Medium Irrespective of Content

A second class of theories is based on the assumption that television as a medium has effects on time use, physical activity, attentional or other cognitive skills, and intellectual effort, in part because of television's inherent audiovisual properties. In discussions based on these theories, television is often contrasted unfavorably with print or with media that are exclusively auditory (e.g., radio).

Time Displacement

One of the most popular hypotheses is that television viewing displaces or takes time away from such intellectually demanding activities as reading or homework (e.g., Koshal, Koshal, & Gupta, 1996; T. M. Williams, 1986), creative and imaginative activities (L. F. Harrison & Williams, 1986; Koolstra & van der Voort, 1996; Valkenburg & van der Voort, 1994), physical activity, and social interaction (MacBeth, 1996; T. M. Williams, 1986).

This happens, according to the hypothesis, because television is higi. attractive to children, presumably more so than participation in othei activities. Not only does television displace concurrent activities and learning opportunities, according to this view, but extensive early experience with television can lead to enduring habits of time use that are both intellectually and physically passive. Turning on the television becomes a habit to relieve boredom, reducing the likelihood that children will find more involving, active pursuits. Not surprisingly, displacement theory predicts generally negative effects of television viewing, especially with respect to cognitive development, academic achievement, and active participation in society.

Television as Default

Time displacement hypotheses are based on the assumption that the overwhelming attraction of television is the cause of reduction in other activities. The default hypothesis, by contrast, states that viewing is the default chosen when other alternatives are not readily available or are not of interest. For example, adolescents who participate in extracurricular activities have less time to watch television; those who are not involved in outside activities have more time at home, where television viewing is a likely way of occupying time. By this view, when time with television is negatively related to time spent in other activities, it is difficult to determine the causal direction. Moreover, processes of displacement and default viewing may both occur.

Synergism of Media

Neuman (1991, 1995) has argued that zero-sum models of time use are too simplistic, positing instead that there are synergistic relations among media. They can be, and often are, used in relation to one another. Children and adults often pursue several activities simultaneously (e.g., play and viewing), and different media are often used in concert with one another (e.g., books and videotapes). Television programs can also provide occasions for social interaction and conversation with peers.

Mental Effort and Passivity

Koolstra and Van der Voort (1996, p. 12) concisely stated a hypothesis common in discussions of television's effects: "that children's pleasant experiences with television lead them to expect that school will be just as amusing. Because this is seldom the case, children lose their enthusiasm

5

for school and school-related activities such as reading." A closely related hypothesis holds that children find television relatively easy to process, whereas other school-relevant activities such as reading are more difficult (Salomon, 1984). Watching television leads to mental laziness, typified by a child who wants to be entertained and is unprepared to invest the mental effort required to master reading or to be creative (Valkenburg & van der Voort, 1994). These hypotheses predict that lowered academic performance and creativity will result from young children's watching of television programming that they find entertaining and easy to understand, regardless of its content.

Theories Based on Television Form

Another set of theories identifies specific features of television form as potential influences on children's intellectual processing or behavior. Some theorists propose that rapid pace and visual and auditory effects lead to superficial intellectual processing. Scene changes and movement, for example, repeatedly elicit orienting reactions that are alleged to induce a passive form of attention to the medium. Images must be processed in rapid succession with little time for reflection. As a consequence, it is argued, children have difficulty sustaining attention in classroom situations, appreciating extended arguments, and thinking creatively (Greenfield, 1984; J. L. Singer, 1980; Valkenburg & van der Voort, 1994).

Some have argued that the visual character of television images interferes with other modes of information processing. In an influential book, Healy (1990) argued that the visual attractiveness of television produces inattention to spoken language, slowing language acquisition and ultimately reducing interest in reading and reading achievement. Greenfield (1994) proposed that the visual nature of television removes the need for the viewer to generate novel images; hence, it is less likely than print or radio to stimulate imagination and creativity.

LONG-TERM OUTCOMES OF EARLY EXPOSURE

The major question addressed in this *Monograph* is whether television exposure at age 5 predicts adolescent achievement, behavior, and attitudes. There are good reasons to expect that early childhood is a period of particular susceptibility to both positive and negative influences of television. Because most American children are not formally schooled until about age 6, television may be a major source of positive content, both preacademic and social. At the same time, both cognitive developmental limitations and lack of background knowledge make it likely that children will incorporate and accept uncritically the content they see (Dorr, 1986; Huesmann & Miller, 1994).

It is unlikely, however, that specific content or media experience at age 5 lead directly to adolescent achievement, behavior, and attitudes. Consequently, any relations of early exposure to adolescent outcomes probably occur through chains of mediators that are activated by early media experiences (MacBeth, 1996; Rosengren & Windahl, 1989; T. M. Williams, 1986). One model for understanding possible long-term effects of early television viewing is based on the hypothesis that media use during the preschool years influences the academic skills, levels of motivation, readiness to learn, and social behavior patterns with which children enter the years of formal schooling, when such behaviors become relatively consistent over time. For example, children who enter school with good skills in the prerequisites for reading, and, to a lesser extent, the prerequisites for math are likely to be placed in higher ability groups and to be perceived as more competent by teachers than children with low levels of preacademic skills. They are also more likely than children without these skills to succeed in the first years of school, leading to a trajectory of further success and positive attitudes about school. These processes have been described as "positive and vicious" circles (Rosengren & Windahl, 1989) or "upward and downward spirals" (T. M. Williams, 1986). There is now a body of evidence showing long-term consequences of experiences in the first grade, particularly ability grouping and differences within classes in teachers' interactions with children (Entwisle, Alexander, & Olson, 1997).

A second, complementary model for understanding long-term effects is based on the understanding that children in the middle childhood and adolescent years play an increasingly important role in their own development through their selection of environments and activities—a phenomenon described as "niche picking" (Scarr & McCartney, 1983) or "reciprocal determinism" (Bandura, 1977). If children's media experiences in early childhood influence their interests, values, and motives or lead them to become more involved in particular activities, they may seek out ways to exercise and enlarge upon those interests. For example, if watching informative television instigates an interest in books, a child may request visits to the library, choose to read or play with books, and gradually become increasingly interested in the world of books.

CAUSAL INFERENCE

The method in this study is correlational, albeit over a span of more than 10 years, from age 5 to ages 15–19. Many of the theories guiding our analyses are based on a model of media "effects," but even when the data support these theories, we cannot infer unidirectional causation. Although the long time span makes it implausible that adolescent behavior affected preschool viewing, individual differences among children could affect both their choice of television at age 5 *and* later teen behavior. In addition, "third variables," including family characteristics, could affect both media use and adolescent behavior. We included controls for parent education, family structure, and site (Massachusetts vs. Kansas) to reduce the likelihood that the results were a function of family characteristics, but there is always the possibility that unmeasured variables influenced both viewing and behavior. As we noted above, however, a unidirectional causal model is not as powerful conceptually as a bidirectional model positing mutual influences of individual characteristics on media use *and* of media on individual interests and behaviors.

SEX DIFFERENCES

Although many individual differences may moderate the relations of media use and behavior, it is especially likely that boys and girls may use and react to television differently. During the years that the adolescents in our study were growing up, television programming of all kinds contained a preponderance of male characters, and in much of the commercial programming, sex-stereotyped behavior patterns were commonly portrayed (Calvert & Huston, 1987). Both surveys and in-depth diary studies have indicated that young boys watch more television than girls, especially cartoons and action-adventure programs containing high levels of violence (Huston & Wright, 1997). By contrast, most studies have found that girls and boys watch about equal amounts of educational programs and are equally attentive to them when they do watch (Anderson & Field, 1983).

Even with equal exposure, however, boys and girls may be differentially susceptible or responsive to the television they experience. Boys in the preschool and school years are generally more vulnerable than girls to low levels of school achievement, behavior problems, and aggression (Golombok & Fivush, 1994). As a result, boys may benefit more than girls from exposure to educational and prosocial programs, and they may be more subject to negative influences of content or form on attention, creativity, and aggression.

Sex stereotypes provoke socialization pressures on boys to be active and aggressive, whereas they lead to experiences that encourage girls to be compliant and cooperative (Golombok & Fivush, 1994). Television messages or influences that go against the grain of sex-stereotyped expectations may have more effect than those that are consistent with other socialization pressures because they are more distinctive in the child's experience. Educational and prosocial messages may have a greater impact on boys than on girls because other developmental influences provide less support for these outcomes among boys. By this reasoning, violent content may have a more negative impact on girls than on boys.

Finally, girls and boys may incorporate and react to different television messages because of different interests and motivations. They may identify with characters of their own sex, pursue different content themes, and incorporate those messages that are particularly relevant to their own motives and interests.

CONCURRENT RELATIONS OF ADOLESCENT MEDIA USE TO BEHAVIOR

Although detailed and comprehensive measurement of preschool viewing makes this study unique, the concurrent relations of adolescent media use to behavior are also of considerable interest. In the fairly large body of literature on adolescent viewing, few studies have classified viewing by type of content, nor have they typically obtained information about the use of different types of print media (e.g., newspapers, magazines, books). Therefore, a secondary purpose of the study was to describe the patterns of adolescent media use and to test predictions regarding the relations of media use to adolescents' patterns of activity in school and outside school, health-related behavior, role models, and images of self.

ORGANIZATION OF THE MONOGRAPH

This study is a survey of 570 adolescents, ages 15–19, whose media use and family characteristics were studied in depth when they were 5 years old. In their adolescence, we obtained measures of media use, academic achievement (including high school transcripts), leisure reading, expectancies of success in school, the value attached to achievement, creativity, extracurricular activities, aggression, health behavior, and self-image. In each of these domains, we derived hypotheses from the major theories of television effects concerning expected adolescent outcomes and evaluated whether the findings supported or refuted them. We contrasted predictions based on media content viewed as a preschooler and as an adolescent with predictions based on time spent with the medium per se. That is, we examined viewing "diets" in preschool and adolescence, usually defined as frequencies of viewing informative, violent, and general entertainment content, and compared each of them with total television time as predictors of adolescent achievement, behavior, and attitudes.

II. METHOD OVERVIEW

In this research we surveyed adolescents who had been preschool participants in one of two studies of television viewing by young children. The goal was to determine the relations of preschool and adolescent television viewing to various characteristics and accomplishments thought to be influenced by television. The adolescents were interviewed by telephone about media use; academic achievement and motivation; participation in extracurricular activities; creativity; aggression; health-related behaviors; and satisfaction with height, weight, and appearance. High school transcripts were obtained for most participants.

The preschool studies took place in Topeka, Kansas (Huston, Wright, Rice, Kerkman, & St. Peters, 1990) and in Springfield, Massachusetts (Anderson, Field, Collins, Lorch, & Nathan, 1985). Although the two studies had different designs and had somewhat different purposes, they employed identical parent-kept viewing diaries and numerous other measures that were the same or similar.

In this report, the dependent variables for the hierarchical regression analyses were derived from the adolescent interviews and the high school transcripts. The main predictor variables were measures of television viewing taken from the preschool viewing diaries, when the participants were 5 years old, and adolescent media use, taken from the interviews. The predictor coefficients were adjusted for background variables including parents' education, research site, birth order, gender, and the interactions of the viewing variables with the background variables.

ADOLESCENT STUDY

Participants

There were 655 children in the two original studies for whom at least one preschool viewing diary was available. Of these, 570 or 87% were

TABLE 1

DEMOGRAPHIC AND BACKGROUND CHARACTERISTICS OF ADOLESCENT SAMPLE
AT TIME OF FOLLOW-UP INTERVIEW

Characteristic	Kansas		Massachusetts		Total	
	Means	SD	Mean	SD	Mean	SD
Father's education	15.56	2.66	15.29	2.94	15.42	2.81
Mother's education	14.93	2.38	14.61	2.49	14.76	2.44
Father's occupational status	4.68	3.74	4.71	3.76	4.70	3.75
Mother's occupational status	4.22	3.18	4.74	3.46	4.50	3.34
Mother's employment hours	33.91	14.42	29.44	16.28	31.58	15.57
Number of older siblings	.32	.59	.39	.64	.36	.62
Number of younger siblings	.89	.98	.78	1.02	.83	1.00
Parents still married (%)	76.3		80.4		78.4	
Age at interview	16.63	1.05	18.21	0.44	17.45	1.12

traced and interviewed (274 or 85.1% of the Kansas sample, 142 males, 132 females; 296 or 88.9% of the Massachusetts sample, 145 males, 151 females). A total of 35 individuals refused to be interviewed (13 Kansas; 22 Massachusetts), and 50 could not be located or had unlisted telephone numbers that informants (such as former neighbors) declined to divulge or did not know (35 Kansas; 15 Massachusetts).[1]

Adolescent Sample Characteristics

The characteristics of the sample at the time of the adolescent interview are summarized in Table 1. The Kansas and Massachusetts samples were comparable on demographic indicators (parent education and occupational status). The Kansas sample was younger than the Massachusetts sample and had a wider range of ages and grade levels. Sixteen percent

[1]Because we did not have social security numbers for parents or children, the effort to contact participants began with the last-known addresses and phone numbers of the families. Methods used included consulting phone books, directory assistance, and high school directories; a Kansas Department of Motor Vehicles (DMV) database search; and using ProCD, a national phone directory on CD-ROM. ProCD allows the user to index searches by last name, address, or phone number. If the parent or child was not listed by ProCD, additional searches were conducted to locate neighbors or relatives using the address search and search by last name, respectively. Phone books, directory assistance, and high school directories combined resulted in 450 participants' being located. Thirty participants were located using the Kansas DMV database search, and 127 participants by using ProCD.

of the total group attended private secondary schools. Participants were almost all European American (ethnicity was not coded; there were fewer than 10 African American participants).

Procedure

Telephone surveys were conducted with most participants between January and May 1994. Individuals who were 18 before September 1, 1993, were contacted first in order to get the information as soon after high school graduation as possible. The remainder of the sample was contacted in alphabetical order, except in cases where tracing was still going on or individuals were difficult to reach.

For each participant, a letter was sent to the adolescent and her/his parent(s) explaining the purposes of the study. The letter was followed by a telephone call to the parent(s). After a brief explanation of the study, the parent was asked to participate in a 5-min interview and, if the adolescent was under 18, to give permission for her/his child to be interviewed. If the parent agreed, a brief interview about family demographics and structure was conducted. Next, the adolescent was interviewed or an appointment was made for an interview. If the adolescent lived away from home, he/she was contacted at his other address by letter and then by telephone. Informed consent by both parent and adolescent was tape-recorded (with permission) before the interview was conducted. The adolescent interview lasted 30–50 min. At its conclusion, the adolescent was told that a letter containing a $10 check and a release form for her/his high school transcript would be sent. Upon return of the release form, whether or not it granted permission to obtain a transcript, another $5 was sent.

Four graduate and undergraduate students at the University of Kansas, who were trained by a lead interviewer, conducted interviews. Quality control was maintained by tape-recording all interviews as backup to the paper records made by the interviewer during the call. The lead interviewer periodically checked randomly selected tapes for procedural fidelity.

Because pilot interviews indicated that viewing patterns and academic indices were quite different for adolescents in high school and those who were not in high school, the 185 (32.5%) adolescents who were not currently in high school were asked retrospective questions about their last (most recent) year in high school. Of these, 153 had graduated and 12 had dropped out of school before graduation. Another 32 were still in high school, but were interviewed during the summer. The validity of these retrospective interviews was assessed; analyses are reported later in this chapter.

Transcripts

High school transcripts were obtained for 491 participants. Of the 570 participants who completed the interview, 520 returned a transcript release form; 29 of these were unsigned. Participants authorizing a request for a transcript attended 79 different schools.

Family and Demographic Measures

Demographic information was collected for the parent respondent with whom the adolescent lived or had most recently lived. It is summarized in Table 1. *Education of parent(s)* was defined as the number of years of education for the parent with whom the teen primarily lived and that parent's spouse or partner. *Occupational status* was based on a job title and number of hours per week of employment obtained for the parent and her/his spouse or partner. Occupational prestige was coded according to a 13-point occupational prestige rating scale developed by Nakeo and Treas (1990) from the 1980 Census Occupational Classification. Job titles were coded as professional/executive (levels 1 and 2 represent executive, managerial, and professional jobs), white collar (levels 3–5 represent technical support, sales, and administrative support), or blue collar (levels 6–13 represent skilled and unskilled trades, service). *Family structure* included parents' marital status, number of siblings in the home, and child's living arrangement. The remaining survey questions are described in the chapters dealing with the topic with which they were concerned.

PRESCHOOL STUDIES

The procedures and measures used in the two preschool studies conducted in the early 1980s are described in detail in Huston et al. (1990) and Anderson et al. (1985).

Participants

Kansas Sample

The initial sample in the Kansas study consisted of 326 children in Topeka, Kansas, who were within 3 months of their third ($N = 160$) or fifth ($N = 166$) birthdays. These children participated in the study for a 2-year period. In addition, there were 20 children who were studied only at age 5. The volunteer sample was recruited through newspaper birth records, preschools, churches, mass media publicity, and posters placed

13

in large office buildings, laundromats, and grocery stores. A staff member attended parent meetings in many venues and visited such places as child care centers to speak to parents and staff. Sign-up sheets were posted in office buildings and preschools; a staff member followed up with a phone describing the study. No effort was made to stratify the sample by population characteristics.

The sample was predominantly European American, and all but 18 families had both parents living in the home at the beginning of the study. Educational level of each parent was coded on a 6-point scale as follows: 1 (*less than high school*), 2 (*high school graduate*), 3 (*some post–high school training*), 4 (*bachelor's degree*), 5 (*some postgraduate training*), 6 (*graduate or professional degree*). For fathers, the mean was 3.78 (*SD* = 1.40); for mothers, the mean was 3.35 (*SD* = 1.23). Occupational status was rated on the Duncan scale, which has a range from 1 to 99 (Duncan, 1961). For fathers, the mean was 52.73 (*SD* = 23.90); for mothers, the mean was 52.18 (*SD* = 18.52). Approximately one third of the mothers were full-time homemakers, one third were employed part time and one third were employed full time. Data were collected from 1981 through 1983.

Massachusetts Sample

A total of 334 families with a child near the fifth birthday were recruited to participate in a study of home television viewing in Springfield, Massachusetts. The study involved the installation of time-lapse video equipment in homes for 10-day periods and maintenance of two 10-day viewing diaries as well as two visits, a month apart, to a child research center. In addition to the 106 families that had video equipment installed in their homes, three comparison groups participated in the study but did not have equipment installed.

Official birth records were used to identify children in the appropriate age range in the community. Families received one of two kinds of letters explaining the study. One letter mentioned the possibility that video equipment would be installed in the home for a 10-day period. The other letter did not mention video equipment. Families recruited with no mention of video equipment constituted one of the comparison groups in order to determine selection effects because of the possibility of home observation (102 families). There were two other comparison groups: 42 families who agreed to have equipment installed but were not asked to do so, and 85 families who initially agreed to have equipment installed but withdrew agreement for the installation of video equipment. All of them agreed to participate in all other portions of the study.

Of the families contacted with no mention of observation equipment in the home, 44.9% agreed to participate in the research. Of the families contacted with mention of observation equipment in the home, 29.9% agreed to participate. The most common reason given for not participating was that the research was too time consuming (14.4% of nonparticipants who received the letters mentioning equipment and 12.2% of nonparticipants who received the alternate letter). Other major reasons given were that the families were not interested in participating in research (12.4% and 12.2%, respectively) and that, because the mother was working, there was not enough time (10.0% and 7.8%, respectively). On 56 questionnaire measures of family demographics, home environment, life stress, attitudes toward television, and others, only two measures indicated a significant difference ($p < .05$) between the groups. This was about what would be expected by chance. Consequently, in the present analyses, we do not distinguish between the families in terms of group status in the original study.

Fathers had completed an average of 15.0 years of schooling ($SD = 2.8$) and mothers an average of 14.2 years ($SD = 2.4$). Families' socioeconomic status (SES) was rated on Hollingshead's Four Factor Index of Social Status (Hollingshead, 1975). The percentages of families in the study at each level were 29% (I), 39% (II), 23% (III), 8% (IV), and 1% (V). The majority of the mothers (63%) were full-time homemakers; 33% had part-time jobs, and 4% were employed full time. Data collection occurred during 1980 and 1981.

Table 2 summarizes the quantitative descriptors of the two preschool samples. Although different scales were used to code parent education and occupational status in the two studies, the samples are demographically comparable. In both samples, parents averaged some post–high school education, and occupational statuses included a wide range, but relatively fewer occupations of lower status than of middle or higher status. Comparisons between those participants who were surveyed (as adolescents) and those who were not are described later in the attrition analyses.

Design and Preschool Measures

Viewing Diaries

The viewing diary used in both studies was a professionally printed form dividing each day into 15-min blocks from 6:00 A.M. to 2 A.M. For each block, the parent was asked to indicate whether the television was on, what channel and program it was tuned to, and who was in the viewing room. Viewing was recorded if the child was in the room while the television set was turned on. Parents were not asked to make a judgment about whether or not the child was "watching" the television because such judgments are considerably more subjective than the report of the child's

TABLE 2

Mean Demographic and Background Characteristics of Preschoolers
Who Were and Were Not Surveyed as Teens

Characteristic	N	Kansas		Massachusetts	
		Surveyed 274	Not surveyed 48	Surveyed 296	Not surveyed 37
Father's educational level[a]		3.82	3.563	15.092	14.270
		(1.33)	(1.382)	(2.799)	(3.159)
Mother's educational level[a]		3.360	3.188	14.304	13.811
		(1.163)	(1.161)	(2.240)	(1.984)
Father's occupational status[b]		53.283	53.854	2.096	2.270
		(23.316)	(23.949)	(0.946)	(0.962)
Mother's occupational status[b]		53.412	51.333	—	—
		(17.751)	(18.472)	—	—
Mother's employment		1.856	2.250***	1.400	1.500
(1 = not, 2 = part, 3 = full)		(0.765)	(0.838)	(0.556)	(0.655)
PPVT-R standard score		107.657	103.854	103.922	104.108
		(12.894)	(14.559)	(13.394)	(13.428)
Hours per week in preschool		11.846	20.943***	8.382	9.297
		(16.135)	(19.865)	(9.559)	(7.717)
Number of siblings		1.360	1.229	1.564	1.513
		(1.067)	(1.292)	(0.986)	(1.216)
Number of younger siblings		.438	.292	.547	.595
		(.497)	(.459)	(.657)	(.686)
Dad lives away from home (%)		7	10***	5	2
Number of working TVs		1.802	1.708	1.814	1.946
		(0.818)	(0.617)	(0.743)	(0.848)
Cable access (0 = none, 1 = basic,		.897	.979	.335	.216
2 = premium channels)		(.866)	(.887)	(546)	(.479)

Note. Entries are means. Standard deviations are in parentheses. Significant differences between those surveyed and not surveyed are indicated by asterisks.
[a]In Massachusetts, entries are years of education. In Kansas, entries are based on a 6-point scale: 1 (*less than high school*), 2 (*high school*), 3 (*some post–high school*), 4 (*college degree*), 5 (*some postgraduate*), 6 (*graduate or professional degree*).
[b]Kansas based on Duncan (1961) scale with range of 1–100; Massachusetts based on Hollingshead (1975) scale with range of 1–5.
***$p < .001$.

presence. Hence, these diaries measured "exposure" to television. In the Massachusetts videotaped observations, children were watching television 67% of the time that they were in its presence. Viewing away from home was recorded on an abbreviated form. A diary was provided for each television set in the household.

The validity of diaries was evaluated in the Massachusetts sample by comparing them with videotaped viewing records for 99 families who had cameras in their homes. Diaries slightly overestimated children's viewing time, but the correlation between the two methods at age 5 was .84, indicating that diaries are a valid method of assessing individual differences. In the Kansas study, validity was also assessed indirectly by examining errors in the diaries (e.g., wrong program title for time and channel listed). Two children were eliminated because their diaries contained large numbers of errors.

In the Kansas study, two cohorts, aged 3 and 5 at the beginning of the study, were followed for a 2-year period. One-week viewing diaries were collected every 6 months (a total of five diaries). All diaries were collected in the spring (March and April) and fall (October and November) to avoid possible extremes of heavy viewing in winter or light viewing in summer.

In the Massachusetts sample, all families completed viewing diaries for two 10-day periods approximately 2 months apart. Diaries were collected throughout the year. Analyses examined amount of reported viewing in relation to the month during which each diary was completed. Viewing levels did not vary systematically as a function of season.

Two diaries were used as the estimate of preschool viewing whenever possible. Because all Massachusetts diaries were collected around the focal child's fifth birthday, the two diaries nearest the fifth birthday in the Kansas sample were included (age 4.5 and 5.0 for the younger cohort, who began the study at age 3; age 5.0 and 5.5 for the older cohort). If only one diary was available, it was used. No children were included who did not have at least one diary from the relevant age periods. Of the Kansas children, 46 children had only one diary and 228 children had two diaries. Of the Massachusetts children, 3 children had only one diary and 293 children had two diaries.

In order to provide for equal representation of each day of the week, viewing estimates for the Massachusetts sample were based on the middle seven (third through ninth) days of data recorded in each diary. The second through eighth days were used in the one diary terminated early by one family (on the eighth day).

Classification of Television Programs

All programs listed in the diaries were classified on four dimensions: (a) *intended audience* (child or general); (b) *informative purpose* (yes or no); (c) *animation* used (full, partial, none); (d) *program type* (news and documentary; sports; comedy; drama; action-adventure and horror; talk, game and variety; CRITC, 1983).

All programs in the *TV Guide* and cable guides for the diary assessment periods in 1981–1983 were initially coded on the basis of raters' knowledge of the series and descriptions in the television guides. Of the

17

5,007 titles in the list, the proportions that could be coded on each dimension were as follows: audience, 95.7%; purpose, 95.9%; animation, 95.1%; program type, 93%. A total of 12 graduate students and staff members served as coders, with the following average interrater agreements on each dimension: audience, 97%; informative purpose, 95%; animation, 98%; program type, 93% (see Huston et al., 1990). Programs viewed by the Massachusetts sample and not by the Kansas sample were subsequently coded using the same system.

For most of the analyses in the follow-up study, the coding dimensions were used to generate three nonoverlapping content categories: *Child informative* programs included all programs designed for a child audience with some intention of providing educational or prosocial content. They included virtually all Public Broadcasting System (PBS) shows for children plus some commercial programs (e.g., *Captain Kangaroo*). *Violent* programs included two program categories that typically have high rates of violence, according to content analyses (Gerbner, Gross, Morgan, & Signorielli, 1994): children's cartoons and general-audience action-adventure. Given the thousands of program titles viewed by our samples, there was no way to code specific content on programs viewed. Although not every cartoon and action-adventure program contains violence (and other program types sometimes show violence), the number of such programs viewed is likely to be a fairly good index of overall exposure to television violence. *Other* programs, primarily entertainment, included child-audience entertainment programs with partial or no animation and general-audience programs. For some analyses, general-audience informative programs (news and documentaries), sports, and other entertainment were separated.

Because child informative programs were of particular interest in the follow-up analyses, we examined exposure to two particular programs in this category, *Sesame Street* and *Mister Rogers' Neighborhood,* because they have been the subjects of extensive commentary about potential effects on development. Table 3 summarizes the preschool viewing data for those participants who were and were not subsequently surveyed in the adolescent study.

Although the original preschool studies were conceived and executed independently of each other, other measures besides the viewing diaries were collected in both. The Peabody Picture Vocabulary Test–Revised (PPVT-R) was administered to all children. The PPVT-R is a standardized instrument measuring receptive vocabulary. It contains norms for ages 2 through adult. It is highly correlated with verbal IQ scores on individual tests of intelligence (Dunn & Dunn, 1981). In the Kansas sample, it was administered at the beginning and the end of the 2-year study. The scores used in the follow-up analyses were those obtained when children were 5 years old, except in 31 cases for which scores were available only at age 3.

TABLE 3

MEAN HOURS OF TELEVISION EXPOSURE PER WEEK BY PROGRAM CATEGORY
FOR PRESCHOOLERS WHO WERE AND WERE NOT SURVEYED AS TEENS

TV Category	N	Kansas		Massachusetts	
		Surveyed 274	Not surveyed 48	Surveyed 296	Not surveyed 37
Sesame Street		2.71	2.33	1.72	1.94
		(2.15)	(2.06)	(1.90)	(1.73)
Child informative		3.96	3.27	4.14	4.80
		(2.74)	(2.57)	(3.61)	(3.41)
Child entertainment (animated)		4.61	4.58	2.98	4.08
		(3.22)	(2.83)	(2.44)	(3.59)
Child entertainment (live)		0.87	1.07	0.56	0.41
		(1.14)	(1.81)	(0.65)	(0.45)
News and documentaries		1.39	1.060	1.017	1.054
		(1.59)	(1.60)	(1.43)	(1.32)
Sports		0.54	0.66	0.34	0.23
		(1.02)	(1.15)	(0.89)	(0.48)
Comedy		3.64	3.79	2.44	3.02
		(3.28)	(2.61)	(2.38)	(2.94)
Drama		1.64	1.70	0.87	1.07
		(1.69)	(2.23)	(1.38)	(1.36)
Action-adventure and horror		1.61	2.05	1.12	0.77*
		(1.63)	(2.29)	(1.21)	(0.78)
Talk, variety, and game shows		0.77	0.69	0.80	0.84
		(1.05)	(1.07)	(0.91)	(0.10)
Unclassifiable		0.24	0.37	1.06	1.706*
		(0.61)	(0.66)	(1.74)	(1.90)
Total hours per week		19.29	19.22	15.33	17.98
		(10.11)	(10.04)	(8.31)	(9.13)

Note. Entries are means. Standard deviations are in parentheses. Significant differences between those surveyed and not surveyed are indicated by asterisks.

*$p < .05$, two-tailed.

Television Focus

One additional measure collected for the Kansas sample was used in the analyses reported here. The child's television focus consisted of parent ratings on 15 items with 5-point Likert-type scales describing how often the child asked questions or talked about television, played television characters and themes, or otherwise brought television content into daily life. The Cronbach alpha for the scale was .82.

METHODOLOGICAL ANALYSES

Attrition Analysis

Attrition analyses were conducted separately by site to determine whether the sample who were interviewed as adolescents was representative of the preschool populations in the original studies. Adolescents who were interviewed were compared with those who were not interviewed on the preschool variables indicated in Tables 2 and 3.

Kansas preschoolers who were not interviewed were more likely to have no father living at home at age 5, to have a mother who worked full time, and to spend more time in child care than individuals who were interviewed. It seems likely that some mothers who were single had re-married and changed their surnames, making the family more difficult to trace. The two groups did not differ significantly on parent education, occupational status, family size, access to cable, or preschool PPVT-R. Television viewing patterns were also similar: Of 24 comparisons, two reached a .05 level of significance. They probably represent chance findings.

Retrospective Validity Analysis

Sample

As noted earlier, 153 of the 570 interviewed teens were not in high school at the time they were interviewed and were given retrospective questions about several of the topics in the interviews. In order to evaluate the validity of these retrospective reports, a sample of 100 participants who were high school seniors at the time of the original interview were reinterviewed approximately 1 year later, when they were no longer in high school.

The sample to be re-interviewed was selected by randomly drawing 100 names from the original 185 high school seniors. An additional 25 names were randomly selected to replace any of the 100 who could not be reached. Of the original 100, 89 completed the retrospective interview. Eleven were replaced for the following reasons: refusal ($n = 3$), could not be located ($n = 1$), could not be reached by phone because of travel or military status ($n = 3$), and could not make telephone contact for other reasons ($n = 4$).

Procedure

The validity interview was an abbreviated, retrospective-format version of the original interview. It took about 15 min. Parents were not interviewed, and, because the adolescents were all 18 or older, parent consent was not required. Participants received a single payment of $10 and a thank-you letter for the retrospective interview.

Retrospective Interview Questions

The interview included retrospective reports of all types of media use (see Chapter 3 for a description of these items), school grades, expectancies of success, perceived utility of academic content (see Chapter 4), future plans, extracurricular activities, and work for the last year in high school (see Chapter 6).

The means obtained in the original and retrospective interviews are shown in Table 4. The differences were significant on 12 of the 39 variables tested. Teens retrospectively overestimated the time spent watching television and time in some activities. They underreported the number of books read and recalled fewer titles of books read the previous year. They judged the content learned in math and science to be less useful and the effort expended in those classes to be less worthwhile. There were no differences in reported high school grades.

Despite these mean differences, the retrospective and original responses were moderately to highly correlated (see Table 4). Thus, although an individual's location in the distribution of original responses might be affected by whether she/he was reporting retrospectively, individual differences were relatively well maintained over a 1-year interval. The retrospective reports were therefore amenable to correction.

To make the necessary correction, individual regression equations (and plots) predicting original survey responses from retrospective ones were calculated for each of the 54 variables of interest. This included generating and examining diagnostic statistics that indexed each point's influence on the regression equation and identifying outliers. Values identified as extremes were deleted, and equations were recomputed. Once the equations were free of the influence of extreme points, they were used to adjust the retrospective responses of the adolescents who had left school before the original interview.

Creativity

The Alternate Uses Test of Divergent Thinking was included in the retrospective interview to provide test-retest reliability. The measure and results are described in Chapter 5.

TABLE 4

ORIGINAL AND RETROSPECTIVE SCORES FOR TEENS REINTERVIEWED
AFTER LEAVING HIGH SCHOOL

Variable	Original		Retrospective		Pearson r
	Mean	SD	Mean	SD	
Total viewing hours per week	10.18	5.68	11.81**	7.27	0.71
News and documentary hours per week	1.85	1.52	1.72	1.32	0.43
VCR hours per week	2.93	3.30	3.29	2.62	0.63
News and talk radio hours per week	2.62	4.23	2.28	3.86	0.37
Weekday paper hours per week	1.87	1.64	1.69	1.65	0.63
Sunday paper hours per month	1.65	1.20	2.21***	1.65	0.57
Magazine hours per month	4.99	10.49	3.80	4.06	0.26
Comic book hours per month	0.35	1.62	0.26	1.56	0.96
Percentage of time English homework done with TV	5.26	17.77	6.69	17.28	0.69
Percentage of time math homework done with TV	4.56	13.60	12.94***	23.86	0.20
Percentage of time science homework done with TV	7.31	19.08	10.48	22.48	0.83
Homework hours per week	7.09	6.73	6.72	5.13	0.59
Number of books read	6.78	8.01	5.23*	7.12	0.54
Number of books could name	3.93	3.11	2.81***	2.37	0.45
Book reading hours per month	8.75	16.13	7.28	11.68	0.39
School-related activity hours per week	7.26	6.46	9.22**	7.74	0.59
Number of school-related activities in the past year	2.64	2.10	2.36	1.97	0.75
Nonschool activity hours per week	3.66	6.42	3.16	4.50	0.55
Number of nonschool activities in the past year	1.07	1.12	1.00	1.02	0.48
Chore hours per week	3.40	3.70	4.15	5.58	0.22
Hours worked for money per week	11.96	9.83	16.21	10.14	0.60
English useful?	3.82	0.90	3.64	1.01	0.44
Math useful?	3.65	1.12	3.45*	1.26	0.65
Science useful?	3.44	1.15	3.16*	1.28	0.55
English effort worthwhile?	3.71	0.92	3.48	1.21	0.37
Math effort worthwhile?	3.83	1.03	3.54*	1.13	0.35
Science effort worthwhile?	3.687‡	1.112	3.29***	1.22	0.45
How good in English?	3.38	0.92	3.36	0.91	0.72
How good in math?	3.17	0.10	3.21	1.07	0.79
How good in science?	3.15	0.97	3.21	1.06	0.64
Compare to others in English?	3.61	0.790	3.69	0.85	0.65
Compare to others in math?	3.59	0.97	3.51	0.99	0.81
Compare to others in science?	3.40	0.85	3.40	0.91	0.68
Advanced English grade predicted	76.89	13.80	77.51	13.76	0.74
Advanced math grade predicted	75.85	14.22	72.62*	19.34	0.66
Advanced science grade predicted	75.24	13.19	74.51	14.68	0.60
English GPA (4-point scale)	3.05	0.69	3.12	0.70	0.87
Math GPA (4-point scale)	2.90	0.66	2.95	0.73	0.72
Science GPA (4-point scale)	3.01	0.73	2.94	0.75	0.69
Overall GPA average of English, math, and science (4-point scale)	2.99	0.55	3.00	0.56	0.87

Note. All correlations were significantly different from zero, $p < .01$, one-tailed. Significant differences between pairs of means in a row all indicated by asterisks, as follows: ‡$p < .10$; *$p < .05$; **$p < .01$; ***$p < .001$, two-tailed.

ANALYSIS PLAN

The major questions addressed throughout this *Monograph* concern the relations of preschool and teen media use to adolescent behavior. Hierarchical multiple regressions were used to test the relations of television exposure to adolescent measures in each developmental domain. A set of covariates was chosen to control for selection effects—that is, for the possibility that covariation between viewing and outcome was due to family or child characteristics. The control variables were sex of respondent, site, parents' education (average), birth order, and the Sex × Site interaction. Sex, parent education, and birth order were included because there was evidence from the preschool studies that they are associated with viewing patterns, and because they were deemed likely to predict such adolescent outcomes as achievement, achievement motivation, and aggression. For example, parent education and birth order are related to both viewing and creativity (Runco, 1991). Site was a necessary control in part because there were age differences between the participants from the two sites.

The second block of variables entered in the regressions contained viewing variables. With the exception of total viewing times, which were distributed approximately normally, the times spent viewing in individual content categories (e.g., child informative, violent), were subject to a transformation (square root of $[x + 1]$) in order to obtain an approximately normal distribution. In most analyses, we tested the viewing diet in preschool (e.g., child informative, violent, other), then added a second block of teen viewing categories (e.g., informative, violent, and other). By including categories that were mutually exclusive and exhaustive, we controlled for total amount of viewing in tests of individual viewing categories.[2] The analyses of preschool viewing tested the long-term prediction from viewing in early childhood to adolescent behaviors; adding teen viewing provided a test of whether a preschool "effect" was mediated by current viewing as well as indicating the concurrent relation of viewing to outcome. Where a hypothesis suggested an effect of total viewing, that was the viewing variable used. In all analyses, we tested for outliers: cases with scores more than three standard deviations from the mean. Analyses were done with and without excluding outliers to be sure that findings were not a function of one or a few extreme scores. Any analysis including outliers that would lead to a different conclusion from the analysis with the outliers deleted is noted in the text.

[2]Models testing one program category at a time were computed for many variables, and the results typically did not differ dramatically from those containing the whole viewing diet.

23

A third block of interactions of Sex × Viewing Category, Site × Viewing Category, and Sex × Site × Viewing Category was tested for all analyses. When these were significant, they are reported, and follow-up analyses were done with subgroups (e.g., separate analyses for males and females if sex appeared in a significant interaction). If they were not significant, the main effects are presented without the interactions.

III. MEDIA USE IN ADOLESCENCE

In this chapter we describe our teenage respondents' use of television, radio, and print media by categories of content, report the correlations among frequencies of using different media, assess the stability of individual differences in television viewing from preschool to adolescence, and examine individual and family characteristics that predict teen media use. Along with the data on preschool media use presented in Table 2, this descriptive information provides a context for understanding the longitudinal analyses of the relations between preschool media use and adolescent characteristics.

REVIEW OF EARLIER RESEARCH ON ADOLESCENT MEDIA USE

Adolescents in industrialized societies spend an average of 1.5 to 2.5 hr per day watching television (Larson & Verma, 1998), which is less than the time spent viewing in late childhood (Comstock & Paik, 1991; Rosengren & Windahl, 1989). These averages are similar across nations in North America and Europe as well as Japan and Korea (Larson & Verma, 1998). In one of the few nonproprietary investigations providing information about what types of programs compose these totals, Swedish adolescents expressed stronger preferences for detective/crime shows, films, and serials than for informational programs (Rosengren & Windahl, 1989). General-audience data in the United States support the supposition that entertainment television constitutes the majority of programs viewed by most adolescents.

Time-use studies show that adolescents in the United States spend an average of .18 to .52 hr per day reading. Teens in Europe and Japan report .33 to .63 hr per day of reading (Larson & Verma, 1998). In two studies, cross-sectional data suggested that reading time increases in early adolescence (Larson, Kubey, & Collectti, 1989; Timmer, Eccles, & O'Brien, 1985). In longitudinal studies of Swedish children, however, time spent reading books declined from fifth to ninth grades, whereas time spent reading magazines and newspapers increased. The contents chosen from newspapers were overwhelmingly sports, comics, and television and radio sections; adolescents reported devoting little attention to print news about politics, domestic, and foreign affairs (Rosengren & Windahl, 1989).

HYPOTHESES ABOUT TELEVISION AND PRINT USE

Among the theories discussed in Chapter 1, the time displacement hypothesis generates the prediction that television viewing leads young people to spend less time reading; hence, one would expect negative correlations between television and print use. Theories emphasizing content lead to the prediction that adolescents will select television and print media with content relevant to their interests and needs (e.g., sports or information; Rosengren, Wenner, & Palmgreen, 1985). Therefore, the content of television and print media should be more important in determining the relations between them than is the total amount of time devoted to either one of them, according to content-based theories.

On the basis of earlier research, we expected differences in media use associated with sex and parent education. Across ages and nations, boys generally watch more television and read fewer books than girls do (Huston & Wright, 1997; Larson & Verma, 1998; Rosengren & Windahl, 1989). The sex differences in television viewing emerge in the preschool years; in part, they reflect the fact that boys watch action-adventure, cartoons, and sports more than girls do (Huston et al., 1990). In industrialized nations, television viewing and print use have opposite associations with SES. Children from families with lower levels of education, occupational status, and income watch more entertainment television and read less than do those in higher SES families (Huston & Wright, 1997; Larson & Verma, 1998; Rosengren & Windahl, 1989; Truglio, Murphy, Oppenheimer, Huston, & Wright, 1996).

MEASURES

Details of the coding and computation of preschool media use variables are provided in Chapter 2. The written diary used in the preschool studies is one of the most valid methods of measuring television use (cf. Anderson & Field, 1991). As it was not possible to obtain such diaries from adolescents during a telephone interview, we devised questions that were designed to elicit accurate estimates of different types of use. In general, respondents are more accurate reporters of media use during specific time periods than they are of overall time estimates. Hence, the questions were designed to assess television use on particular days of the week or during particular time intervals. One difference between the preschool and adolescent measures was assessment of "exposure" in preschool (i.e., time in the presence of an operating television set) as opposed to assessment of "viewing" in adolescence (however the respondent defined that term). For the preschool children, videotapes of home viewing showed that individual differences in exposure time were reasonable indicators of individual differences in actual viewing. There was no systematic difference in attentiveness for children who were frequently and infrequently exposed to television (Anderson & Field, 1983).

Television Viewing

For each of the seven weekdays, the adolescent was asked "How much time do you spend watching television on a typical (day of week)?" and "What programs do you usually watch on (day of week)?" *Total weekly viewing time* was the sum of time estimates for the 7 days.

Each of the television programs mentioned was classified by content category. *Informative* programs were news, documentaries, nature shows, and other programs supplying information about the real world outside of television. *Violent* programs were cartoons and action-adventure shows. For most analyses, all other programs were grouped as *general entertainment*. For some analyses, *sports* were tallied separately. Participant reports of viewing time on a particular day did not always equal the total broadcast time of the programs reported as typically viewed on that day. Therefore, the number of programs named in each of the program types was converted to a proportion of all programs named. The estimate of viewing time for each category was this proportion multiplied by the total weekly reported viewing time, yielding exposure scores for each program category.

For the remaining questions about television and other media, a two-part format was used. The first question was "How many days a week (or a month) do you do (activity)?" The second was "On the days when you do (activity), how much time do you spend doing that?" The answers were multiplied to calculate total time per week or per month. This format was used to ask about watching news or documentaries, watching videotapes, and listening to news or talk radio.

Print Use

Using the same two-part format, participants were asked how often they read books not required for school. They were also asked how many books not required for school they had read during the previous year and the titles and authors of several of the books read during the prior year. Each of these variables was subjected to a square-root transformation before generating z scores. The intercorrelations were .49 for hours with number named, .61 for hours and number in the past year, and .44 for number in the past year with number named, all $ps < .001$. An aggregate index of book use was created by averaging z scores for these three indicators. This aggregate was correlated .85, .83, and .78 (all $ps < .001$) with number of book hours, books named, and books read in the past year, respectively.

Teens were asked two-part questions about how often they read weekly and Sunday newspapers, comic books, and magazines. For magazines, they were asked what titles they read. Titles were coded as *media-related* (entertainment magazines that highlight celebrities or music figures/information and glamour magazines that promote beauty, fashion or style), *real public world* (news and information), *sports* (featuring group/team sports, individual sports, and fitness), and *other*. The proportion of exposure to different categories of magazines was calculated by dividing the number of magazines in a particular category by the total number of magazines named by the respondent. The total hours per month was then multiplied by the proportion of exposure to yield the number of hours per month spent reading magazines in a particular category.

For participants who were not currently in high school or who were interviewed during the summer, all of the media questions were retrospective. They were asked to recall their media use during their last year in high school. The reliability of these measures and adjustment for retrospective bias is reported in Chapter 2.

RESULTS

Media Use

Television Viewing

Teens reported viewing an average of 11.13 hr of television per week (Table 5). One measure of time spent on different types of programs was calculated from the proportion of program titles named in reports of daily viewing. By this measure, over half of the time was devoted to general entertainment programming, and a little over an hour was devoted to informative programs.

A second measure of informative viewing was based on questions about how often participants watched news or documentaries; according to this index, teens watched slightly over 2 hr a week of informational programs.

TABLE 5

DESCRIPTIVE INFORMATION ABOUT ADOLESCENTS' USE OF TELEVISION,
RADIO, AND PRINT MEDIA

Category	All		Male		Female	
	Mean	SD	Mean	SD	Mean	SD
Television						
Informative titles[a]	1.22	2.10	1.18	2.11	1.25	2.10
Violent titles[a]	1.25	2.73	1.54	3.13	.95	2.23**
Sports titles[a]	2.13	3.90	3.48	4.84	.76	1.79***
Other titles[a]	6.52	5.23	6.13	5.06	6.92	5.38***
Total time[a]	11.13	7.16	12.33	7.61	9.90	6.47**
Documentary frequency[a]	2.10	1.76	2.33	1.98	1.87	1.47
VCR frequency[a]	2.96	3.26	3.38	4.14	2.52	1.92**
Radio						
Radio news/talk[a]	2.75	4.86	2.42	3.86	3.09	5.69
Newspapers						
Weekday[a]	1.60	1.30	1.76	1.43	1.44	1.15**
Sunday[b]	1.30	1.17	1.47	1.25	1.12	1.10**
Books						
Comics[b]	0.41	3.00	.75	4.20	.07	.25
Hours reading[b]	10.03	19.36	8.97	16.70	11.10	21.70
Number read in last year	10.61	27.78	7.70	15.74	13.58	35.92
Number could name	3.82	2.80	3.65	2.76	4.00	2.83
Book use index	.00	2.39	−.19	1.90	.20	2.79
Magazines						
All[b]	4.80	7.59	5.25	9.15	4.35	5.57
Entertainment[b]	1.94	4.73	.78	4.10	3.11	5.03***
News/information[b]	1.37	3.56	1.62	4.10	1.13	2.90
Sports[b]	.75	1.88	1.26	2.13	.24	1.41***

Note. Tests of differences between males and females were performed in regression analyses reported in Table 6.
[a]Entries are hours per week.
[b]Entries are hours per month.
**$p < .01$. ***$p < .001$.

The correlation between this direct question and the index based on programs named (with gender controlled) was .39 ($p < .001$). Teens reported watching almost 3 of the 11 hr per week on a VCR and listening to news and talk radio an average of 2.75 hr per week.

Print Use

Teens reported spending about 10 hr per month reading books not assigned in school, or approximately .33 hr per day. This is again consistent with levels reported in prior research. The variability was very large;

28.1% of respondents reported no book reading in the prior month, and others reported large amounts. Respondents said they had read an average of about 10 books in the last year, and they named about 3.5 titles on average. They reported spending 5 hr per month reading magazines. The teens reported spending about 8 hr per month reading newspapers and less than 1 hr reading comic books (see Table 5).

Sex, Family Characteristics, and Site as Predictors of Adolescent Media Use

Each of the media use variables except comic book reading was regressed on parent education, birth order, sex, site, and Sex × Site. Because the participants in the two sites differed in age, a second set of regressions was run using age instead of site, but the results were substantially the same and are not presented. Those dependent variables on which the total R^2 reached $p < .05$ are shown in Table 6.

Individual and family characteristics were associated with media use in ways that are consistent with other literature. Adolescents whose parents had relatively low levels of education spent slightly greater amounts of time watching television of all kinds and less time reading books or news magazines. Higher levels of parent education were associated with being able to name books read in the last year and reading news and information magazines, but not with other indicators of print use. Birth order accounted for relatively little variance in media use.

The most pronounced individual differences were associated with sex. Males reported watching more television overall than females (see Table 5). Males watched more television of almost every category and, not surprisingly, used both video and print media associated with sports more than females did. Females read magazines about media and entertainment figures, including fashion models, more than males did. These differences are consistent with the notion that teens' media use is guided in part by sex-stereotyped interests.

There were few differences associated with site. Massachusetts teens, who were on average older than Kansas teens, reported more time reading daily newspapers but less time reading Sunday newspapers or watching documentaries. For total viewing and for viewing entertainment programs, the interaction of Sex × Site was significant. The sex differences were larger for the Massachusetts sample than for Kansas teens.

Relations Among Frequencies of Using Different Media

The correlations among reported frequencies of using different media are shown in Table 7. Because there were sex differences in many

TABLE 6

SUMMARY OF REGRESSION ANALYSES PREDICTING ADOLESCENT MEDIA USE FROM FAMILY AND INDIVIDUAL CHARACTERISTICS

A. Television

Predictor	Total	Violent	Entertainment	Sports	Documentary	VCR
Parent education	-.11**	-.07	-.11**	-.06	.03	-.08
Birth order	.03	-.04	.04*	.03	-.02	-.01
Sex (female)	-.19***	-.12**	-.20***	-.39***	-.05	-.13**
Site (MA)	.06	.06	.06	.05	-.13**	-.03
Sex × Site	.12**	-.01	.10*	0	-.01	.03
Adjusted R^2	.061***	.014*	.059***	.145***	.015*	.017*

B. Print Media

Predictor	Newspapers		Books		Magazines	
	Weekly	Sunday	Number named	Entertainment	News/ Informative	Sports
Parent education	.06	-.02	.14**	-.07	.11**	.07
Birth order	-.03	-.05	-.07	.00	-.04	.03
Sex (female)	-.13**	-.14**	.06	.24***	-.07	-.27***
Site (MA)	.26***	-.10*	.06	.04	.04	.06
Sex × Site	-.02	-.01	-.04	.06	-.07	.00
Adjusted R^2	.076***	.026**	.025**	.064***	.026*	.074***

Note. Entries are standardized regression coefficients and adjusted R^2. For the following dependent variables, the adjusted R^2 values were not significant, so results are not reported in the table: informative television, radio news and talk, magazines, books read (hours), books read (#), book use index.

*p < .05. **p .01. ***p < .001.

TABLE 7
Partial Correlations Among Categories of Teen Media Use (Gender Controlled)

Television	Informative	Violent	Entertainment	Sports	Documentary	VCR	Radio News/Talk
Total	.26**	.41**	.54**	.42**	.29**	.36**	.09
Informative	—	.07	-.35**	-.04	.39**	.14**	-.02
Violent		—	-.31**	-.12**	.14**	.29**	.06
Other entertainment			—	.49**	-.02	.11**	.05
Sports				—	.21**	.09**	.04
Documentary					—	.00	.17***
VCR						—	.03

	Newspapers		Books				Magazines			
	Daily	Sunday	(hours)	# read	# named	Book use	All	Entertainment	News/inform	Sports
Television and radio										
Total TV	.01	.09*	.17**	.05	-.01	.09	.02	.05	-.01	.06
Informative	-.03	.13**	.07	.04	.03	.06	.05	.04	.07	-.09*
Violent	-.04	.06	.22**	.16**	.09*	.20**	.02	.01	.03	-.03
Other entertainment	-.06	-.01	-.06	-.04	-.12**	-.12**	-.02	.03	-.08*	.14**
Sports	.15**	.05	-.05	-.04	.07	-.01	-.01	-.02	-.08	.25**
Documentary	.12**	.17**	.04	.00	.04	.03	-.08	-.01	.06	.02
VCR	-.04	.08*	.09*	.03	-.03	.04	-.03	-.02	-.05	.03
Radio news/talk	-.01	.02	.13**	.02	-.07	.03	.05	-.05	-.05	.03
Daily paper	—	.30**	-.04	.00	.12**	.07	.08	-.03	.21**	.24**
Sunday paper		—	.06	.03	.07	.07	.24**	.12**	.13**	.12**
Books (hr/month)			—	.66**	.39**	.85**	.12**	.04	.08	-.02
Number of books read				—	.30**	.82**	.10*	.10*	.05	-.04
Number of books named					—	.71**	.06	.01	.14**	.07
Book use (composite)						—	.12**	.06	.11**	.00
Total magazines							—	.64**	.52**	.25**
Entertainment (hr/month)								—	.18**	-.04
News/informative (hr/month)									—	.19**

*p < .05. **p < .01.

forms of media use, sex was partialed out of these correlations. The total amount of television viewed was, by definition, associated with subcategories of television but was not related to radio use and was only weakly related to use of print media. Contrary to displacement-theory predictions, the few significant correlations of television viewing with print use (reading the Sunday paper and reading books) were slightly positive.

Compared to adolescents who reported watching relatively little informational programming, those who reported watching informative television titles or who said they often watched documentaries were less likely to watch entertainment television and more likely to listen to news and talk radio and to read newspapers. There was no relation of informative television viewing to reading books or magazines.

Those who watched more violent programs watched *less* general entertainment and sports, and they reported watching *more* documentaries and videotapes as well as *more* book reading than did low viewers of violent programs. This pattern may reflect an attraction to dramatic narrative or complex plots for these teens. Many of the most complex dramas fall in the violent action-adventure category.

Teens who watched a lot of general entertainment, by contrast, watched a lot of sports and read sports magazines but reported less book use than did those who watched less general entertainment programming. Teens who often watched sports on television reported reading the daily newspaper and sports magazines but not other print media, possibly because they followed newspaper and magazine reports of sports events.

The correlations among different types of print use indicated that teens who read newspapers also read magazines, but reading books was relatively independent of using other types of print media. Youth who read news magazines also reported reading other categories of magazine, but there was no relation between reading entertainment and sports magazines.

Preschool Viewing as a Predictor of Adolescent Television Use

The correlations of preschool with adolescent viewing, with sex partialed out, are shown in Table 8. All three categories of preschool viewing (informative, violent, and other) were modestly but positively associated with total viewing in the teen years. More interesting is the evidence of some stability within program type. Children who often watched violent programs at age 5 reported watching more violent, sports, and general entertainment programs as adolescents than did other respondents. Many of the programs that formed the violent category at age 5 were cartoons; by adolescence, the majority of violent programs viewed were action-adventure shows. Children with relatively heavy diets of general

TABLE 8

<small>Stability of Viewing: Correlations of Preschool With Teen Television Use (Gender Controlled)</small>

| Teen television viewing | Preschool television viewing | | | |
	Informative	Violent	Other entertainment	Total
Total	.08*	.19**	.12**	.25**
Informative	.05	.06	.03	.10*
Violent	.08	.09*	.01	.10*
Other entertainment	.01	.11**	.10*	.13**
Sports	−.02	.09*	.08*	.08

*$p < .05.$ **$p < .01.$

entertainment programs at age 5 watched more "other" entertainment and sports programming in the teen years.

CONCLUSIONS

The teens in this sample watched between 1.5 and 2.0 hr of television per day, a figure that is consistent with the lower range of viewing reported by Larson and Verma (1998). Similarly, as expected, teens with more-educated parents watched less entertainment television and read more books and magazines that those with less-educated parents. There were significant sex differences in many aspects of media use, and most of these were consistent with sex-typed interests and preferences. Males watched more violence and sports on television, and they read more newspapers and sports magazines. Females watched more general entertainment and read more entertainment magazines (those that featured media figures, romance, and the like). It is noteworthy that there were not significant sex differences in reading books, perhaps because the within-group variability for both sexes was quite large.

The clustering of media use patterns does not support the time-displacement hypothesis but is consistent with the idea that it is not so much the medium—television or print—as the potential uses, interest value, or functions of particular content that are important. Teens who read newspapers also watched television news and documentaries, listened to radio news and talk shows, and read news magazines. Those who watched sports television also read newspapers and sports magazines but were not especially likely to read books. Those who watched violent television also watched documentaries and read books (presumably novels). These patterns support theories emphasizing that viewers actively use media to fulfill particular functions: They choose a range of media to obtain information, to follow their interests, or to find their preferred types of entertainment.

Individual differences in the amount of television viewing were modestly stable from preschool to the teen years, and there was some stability of program choices. Stability of viewing patterns may reflect individual differences in preferences and interests that last over time, but it may also result from continuity in the home environment. What others in the family watch influences children's viewing, and those influences may themselves have stability over time.

SUMMARY

Teens reported watching a little over 11 hr a week of television, about half of which was general entertainment programming. Males watched more violent and sports television and more documentaries and read more newspapers and sports magazines; females watched more entertainment television and read more entertainment magazines. There was modest consistency in viewing patterns from preschool to adolescence. Teens' use of different media (television and print) appeared to be based on content rather than the type of medium (i.e., television vs. print).

IV. ACADEMIC ACHIEVEMENT

In Chapters 2 and 3, we presented descriptive information about preschool and adolescent media use. In this and subsequent chapters, we test relations of preschool and teen viewing diet to adolescent behavior, motivation, and attitudes. We begin in this chapter with an examination of academic achievement.

Children's television viewing is often claimed to be harmful to academic achievement. Acting on this claim, a national organization (TV Free America) promotes a television-free week every April in order to foster healthy child development. The American Academy of Pediatrics recommends that parents permit no television viewing by children under 2 years of age, regardless of the program (Mifflin, 1999).

In seeming contradiction, television is considered by many to be a powerful medium for educating children. In the early days of television, many people expected and hoped that the medium would be a source of stimulation and enrichment. It soon became clear that, without special effort, commercially supported television was not generally educational. Explicitly educational programming drew small, elite audiences.

In the late 1960s, *Sesame Street* became the pioneering example of a new generation of curriculum-based television programs. It was developed on the assumption that sophisticated and professional television production techniques would be necessary to gain an audience in competition with commercial entertainment television (Lesser, 1972). Beginning with its first broadcast in 1969, *Sesame Street* quickly gained a large audience of preschool children, and, after more than 30 years, it remains one of the most popular programs for preschool children in the United States and internationally.

During the 1970s and 1980s, however, fears steadily intensified concerning the negative influence of television on cognitive development and academic achievement. A trade book, *The Plug-In Drug* (Winn, 1977), which has gone through at least one revision and many printings, argued that television stultifies cognitive development and displaces intellectually valuable activities. These arguments were repeated and extended in various other popular books and magazine articles (e.g., Healy, 1990; Mander, 1978; Moody, 1980; J. L. Singer & Singer, 1979; Winn, 1987). *Sesame Street*, despite its educational goals, was the focus of many of the concerns. The program's use of production techniques common in entertainment television fostered fears that children would fail to develop the ability to sustain attention in formal educational situations. This attitude is captured in the following quote from Healy (1990, p. 219): "The worst thing about *Sesame Street* is that people believe it is educationally valuable." These beliefs were bolstered by a critical reanalysis of the original summative evaluations of *Sesame Street*, concluding that the positive effects were primarily limited to middle-class children and were due to mediation by parents (Cook et al., 1975).

HYPOTHESES BASED ON CONTENT

In this section, we summarize hypotheses drawn from the general theories presented in Chapter 1, and we evaluate existing research concerning the relations of television viewing to academic achievement. More complete reviews may be found elsewhere (Anderson & Collins, 1988; Comstock & Paik, 1991; Hornik, 1981; Huston & Wright, 1997; MacBeth, 1996; Morgan & Gross, 1982; Neuman, 1991, 1995). We begin with hypotheses based on theories emphasizing content and then present those emphasizing qualities of the medium.

Early Learning Hypothesis

Observational learning and information processing theories lead to the straightforward prediction that children can learn the content presented on television. When the participants in this study were 5 years old, they could watch such child informative programs as *Sesame Street, Mister Rogers' Neighborhood,* and *Captain Kangaroo,* which were explicitly designed to convey cognitive and social curricula to preschoolers. They could also watch *3-2-1 Contact, Electric Company, In the News,* and *Schoolhouse Rock,* which were designed for school-aged children. Numerous studies indicated that viewers learned the intended curricula of these programs (see Bryant, Alexander, & Brown, 1983). For example, viewers of *Mister Rogers' Neighborhood* learned and practiced the prosocial behaviors stressed in that show (see Stein & Friedrich, 1975).

Sesame Street was one of the few educational programs emphasizing cognitive and language skills (Neapolitan & Huston, 1994). Initial summative evaluations using random-assignment experimental designs demonstrated that the program achieved its goal of providing children with skills relevant to early success in school (Ball & Bogatz, 1970; Bogatz & Ball, 1972). An analysis of the National Household Education Survey revealed that preschool *Sesame Street* and *Reading Rainbow* viewers were "more likely to be able to count to twenty, identify the primary colors by name, and show other signs of emerging literacy and numeracy than their counterparts who were not current viewers of the program" (Zill, Davies, & Daly, 1994, p. 20). First and second graders who watched *Sesame Street* before entering school "were more likely to be reading storybooks on their own and less likely to be receiving special help in school for reading problems" (Zill et al., 1994, p. 20). Among children from lower-income families, viewing *Sesame Street* at ages 2 and 3 positively predicted vocabulary and math skills and school readiness at age 5 (Wright et al., in press). In all of these studies, the relations of viewing to academic skills occurred after controlling for a variety of family characteristics.

The evidence is slightly more mixed for educational programs in general, perhaps because the content and quality is variable. In a longitudinal study of Swedish children, frequent viewers of "children's" programs (most of which were probably informative) in preschool performed better on grade 1 tests of letter knowledge, number knowledge, reading, spelling, and spatial ability and had better marks in grade 6. Children who often watched "fictional" programs (which were presumably less educational) in preschool had lower marks in grade 6 (Jonsson, 1986; Rosengren & Windahl, 1989). By contrast, Koolstra and Van der Voort (1996) found that television viewing predicted reduced reading skill among Dutch children from grades 2 through 8 and that this finding held true for each of four kinds of programs (entertainment, drama, informational, and children's programs). This is the only study that has found a negative relation between informational viewing and school-relevant achievement. It should be noted that their category of informational programs was not defined and may have primarily consisted of programs for adults.

Insofar as early child informative viewing prepares children for school and helps ensure initial success and positive school experiences, as suggested by most of the research, it may lay the foundation for long-term academic achievement by influencing cognitive skills, social behavior, and motivation to achieve. As noted in Chapter 1, there is evidence that children's academic and behavioral skills in first grade have important consequences for placement in ability groups and for teachers' perceptions, which in turn set children on trajectories of later success or failure in school (Entwisle et al., 1997).

Such early success may also increase children's motivation and confidence. According to expectancy-value theory, the motivation to succeed in a particular domain is a function of *expectancy* of success or beliefs about one's own competence and the *value* attached to success (Eccles, Wigfield, & Schiefele, 1997). Television might influence these components of success directly, by teaching content or stimulating interests, or indirectly, through its impact on school success.

Violence Viewing Hypothesis

A second hypothesis, derived from information processing theory, is that violent television will have indirect negative effects on academic achievement through its impact on aggression (Huesmann & Eron, 1986). Aggressive behavior can lead to spirals of lower output, lower quality of work, poorer grades, reduced motivation to succeed, and a negative cycle of academic failure and alienation from the culture of achievement and the goals represented by the educational system (T. M. Williams, 1986; MacBeth, 1996).

There is abundant evidence that early aggressive behavior patterns are associated with subsequent poor school achievement (e.g., Bates, Petit, & Dodge, 1995; Kokko & Pulkkinen, 2000). There is also longitudinal evidence that children who watch violent television frequently perform less well in school than do other children (Huesmann & Eron, 1986). This correlation could, of course, indicate that violence viewing affects achievement or that low achievers select violent programs. A 22-year longitudinal study indicated that reduced academic achievement was more likely a consequence than an antecedent of violence viewing (Huesmann, Eron, Lefkowitz, & Walder, 1984). Moreover, well-educated parents watched more violence than less well-educated parents, suggesting that violent programming is not simply the choice of poor achievers (Huesmann & Eron, 1986).

HYPOTHESES BASED ON TELEVISION AS A MEDIUM

Time Displacement

According to the time-displacement hypothesis, television viewing leads children and youth to spend reduced time on school-related activities, especially reading and homework, and cultivates habits of intellectual passivity that are antithetical to high achievement. At first blush, this prediction appears to be supported. Numerous state and national assessments have reported negative correlations of time spent with television and educational achievement. The size of the relation, however, is small. In reviewing 23 such assessments comprising 277 correlations of television viewing and achievement, P. A. Williams, Haertel, Walberg, and Haertel (1982) reported a median correlation of –.06. Moreover, the relation was in fact curvilinear, with the students who averaged about 10 hr per week showing higher achievement than those reporting less viewing. For times greater than 10 hr per week, the median correlation was –.09.

The associations between viewing and achievement are at least partly a function of such factors as greater parental education and higher economic status that are associated with low levels of viewing and high academic achievement. When the data are broken down by educational or professional status of the parents, however, negative relations between amount of television viewing remain within broadly defined social groups, especially middle and upper middle SES (Comstock & Paik, 1991). For children from lower SES families, studies find either no relation between viewing and achievement (e.g., Keith, Reimers, Fehrmann, Pottebaum, & Aubey, 1986), or a positive relation (e.g., Fetler, 1984).

There is some evidence that the introduction of television in a society interferes with reading acquisition, but the effect appears to be a temporary "novelty bubble" affecting only those engaged in initial acquisition of reading at the time (Corteen & Williams, 1986; Hornik, 1978). In these special cases, television may be sufficiently attractive that it overwhelms the young child's interest in reading. With television well established, however, three longitudinal studies with controls for individual and family characteristics show little or no relation of television viewing to reading or math achievement. Gaddy (1986) found television viewing unrelated to reading, vocabulary, or math achievement from grades 10 to 12, and, in a large sample, television viewing did not predict reading or mathematics achievement from ages 6 to 11 years (Gortmaker, Salter, Walker, & Dietz, 1990). Television viewing did not predict reading ability or reading time (after application of controls) from grade 2 through grade 8 (Ritchie, Price, & Roberts, 1987; Roberts, Bachen, Hornby, & Hernandez-Ramos, 1984).

It might be argued that displacement is critically important during the preschool years. Burton, Calonico, and McSeveney (1979) reported that amount of preschool television viewing (retrospectively estimated by parents) was negatively related to first-grade achievement. On the other hand, better controlled longitudinal research across the preschool years found no relation between general entertainment viewing and vocabulary development, whereas *Sesame Street* viewing positively predicted vocabulary increase (Rice, Huston, Truglio, & Wright, 1990). This latter result suggests that content viewed may be the controlling factor.

Even the weak negative relations between overall viewing and achievement may be a function of television content. In an analysis of state assessment data from California grade 6 students, light viewers had higher achievement scores than heavy viewers, but total amounts of viewing were confounded with content viewed. Heavy viewers reported viewing entertainment programs, and light viewers reported viewing informational programs (Fetler, 1984). Similarly, in a study of 8th- through 12th-grade students, Potter (1987) found that although some entertainment categories of viewing were negatively associated with achievement, viewing informational television was positively associated with achievement.

Even if low achievement were associated with high television viewing time, that does not, of course, show that time displacement is necessarily the underlying cause. First, not all time spent with television displaces other activities (e.g., Anderson & Field, 1991; Bechtel, Achelpohl, & Akers, 1972; Timmer et al., 1985). Second, time spent with television does not displace substantial amounts of cognitive and educational activity. Landmark studies during the early days of television concluded that time spent with television primarily displaced time spent with functionally similar entertainment media—movies, radio, comic books, and pulp magazines (Himmelweit, Oppenheim, & Vince, 1958; Schramm, Lyle, & Parker, 1961). Leisure time book reading was not generally affected, because as Hornik (1981, p. 202) noted, "there was not much reading before television, and there is not much now." Similarly, when television was introduced in South Africa, 7th- through 12th-grade children reduced their reading by less than 3 min per day and homework by about 0.5 min per day (Mutz, Roberts, & Van Vuuren, 1993).

Once television became firmly established, researchers found inconsistent results with respect to the relations of reading and television time (Medrich, Roizen, Rubin, & Buckley, 1982; Timmer et al., 1985). Similarly, there is little evidence of a trade-off between time spent with television and time spent doing homework (e.g., Keith et al., 1986). Even when negative correlations occur, the direction of cause and effect is impossible to determine. For example, families who do not value literary activities may implicitly or explicitly encourage television viewing instead of reading. If television were unavailable, it is not clear that more reading would occur.

Although television viewing in general does not clearly displace valuable activities, it is possible that the content viewed may be important with respect to displacement of reading and other educational activities. Huston, Wright, Marquis, and Green (1999), in a longitudinal study of 2- to 7-year-olds, traced individual patterns of change in time use over a 3-year time span. As viewing of general entertainment programming increased, children spent less time in reading and educational activities, social and outdoor activities, and video game play; conversely, declines in viewing were associated with increases in these other activities. There was no relation, however, between changes in time spent viewing educational programs and time spent in other activities. These results suggest that if a negative impact of time displacement exists, it is associated with the time spent viewing entertainment content rather than educational content.

Time displacement thus has a plausible but unproven impact on cognitive development and academic achievement. It is clear, however, that the theory makes a straightforward prediction: Time spent watching television, regardless of its content, should be negatively related to academic achievement.

Attention Hypothesis

As discussed in Chapter 1, many scholars and teachers believe that television shortens the attention span of children because of its rapid visual pacing and the lack of interaction involved (e.g., J. L. Singer, 1980). Frequent elicitation of the orienting reaction by movement and cuts is theorized to encourage passive and inappropriate forms of attention and cognition. This theory leads to the hypothesis that *Sesame Street*'s magazine format and use of sophisticated visual production techniques will lead to poor academic performance and to less time in such sustained activities as reading books. The attention hypothesis is widely held; some even consider television a source of attention-deficit disorder (Hartmann, 1996).

Sudden visual changes on television do elicit orienting reactions (e.g., Rothschild, Thorsen, Reeves, Hirsch, & Goldstein, 1986), but there is little research support for other aspects of the theory. There is no evidence for either negative effects of television in general or *Sesame Street* in particular on children's ability to sustain attention, although there is evidence that violent content may lead to impulsive behavior (for reviews, see Anderson & Collins, 1988; MacBeth, 1996). In fact, educational programs such as *Sesame Street* and *Mister Rogers' Neighborhood* are associated with positive effects (especially those episodes that attempt to teach attention strategies), whereas violent action programs are associated with negative effects, perhaps because of modeling of impulsive behavior. In the only study to examine the effects of *Sesame Street*'s pacing directly, no effects of rapid versus slow pacing were found on perseverance, impulsivity, or sustained play (Anderson, Levin, & Lorch, 1977).

However, Koolstra and Van der Voort (1996) presented a longitudinal analysis of the relation between television (including informational programs) and book reading by Dutch children in grades 2 and 4 indicating that television may reduce book reading. Their analysis indicated that television reduces concentration during reading, but their measure of concentration was based on children's self-ratings rather than on direct observation. This is the only study that provides evidence of a negative effect consistent with the attention hypothesis. It should be pointed out that other longitudinal studies across the same age range, reviewed earlier in the context of displacement theory, did not find a negative relation between television viewing and time spent reading.

Language Deficit Hypothesis

In an influential book, Healy (1990) argued that television, and *Sesame Street* in particular, induces inattention to action and dialogue and thus retards children's language development and reduces reading ability (see Chapter 1). Children do selectively attend to video when audio and video tracks are mismatched (Hayes & Birnbaum, 1980). If the audio and video are consistent, however, children are more likely to recall dialogue than if there is no accompanying video, suggesting that the video actually enhances attention to dialogue (Gibbons, Anderson, Smith, Field, & Fischer, 1986).

In fact, there is no evidence that television interferes with vocabulary acquisition. In the early 1950s children in towns with television had *more* (not less) advanced vocabularies than children in towns without television (Schramm, Lyle, & Parker, 1961). In the 1970s, there were no differences in vocabulary acquisition between those who lived in a Canadian town without television and those in two towns with television (L. F. Harrison & Williams, 1986). Rice and Woodsmall (1988) showed that children readily learn vocabulary from brief exposure to a children's television program, and Rice et al. (1990) found that *Sesame Street* viewing predicted increases in vocabulary from ages 3 to 5.

In summary, no research has found that television viewing is associated with reduced language development. Nevertheless, the language deficit hypothesis has received a great deal of press coverage, and a major government-sponsored conference was organized in the early 1990s to explore Healy's ideas (Clark & King, 1992). The hypothesis most clearly predicts that viewing television, particularly *Sesame Street,* should be associated with reduced achievement, especially in English, as well as reduced book reading, whereas the evidence suggests, if anything, the opposite.

Entertainment and Mental Effort Hypothesis

On slightly different grounds, both Koolstra and Van der Voort (1996) and Salomon (1984), along with many authors of popular books and articles on television, proposed that television can lead children to prefer easy, undemanding activities that require relatively little mental effort (see Chapter 1). Hence, they predict that viewing any television programming that is easy to understand and entertaining (including educational programs) will have negative consequences.

43

To our knowledge, Koolstra and Van der Voort (1996) provide the only test of this hypothesis. In their longitudinal study of second- through eighth-grade Dutch children, television viewing was associated with a subsequent decrease in positive attitudes toward reading. Attitudes toward reading, in turn, predicted reading achievement and time spent reading. They considered this finding consistent with the entertainment hypothesis.

Children do rate television as requiring less mental effort than reading (Beentjes, 1989; Salomon, 1984). Roberts et al. (1984), moreover, found that rated mental effort in reading was positively associated with reading achievement. On the other hand, "children who perceived television as an easy means for learning about things tended to obtain higher reading achievement scores" (p. 36). In their longitudinal study of Dutch children, Koolstra and Van der Voort (1996) reported a causal analysis that failed to provide support for the mental effort hypothesis insofar as television viewing did not predict subsequent estimates of the mental effort involved in reading.

Although the evidence to date is somewhat equivocal, the entertainment and mental effort hypothesis clearly predicts that early television viewing should be negatively associated with later leisure book reading and with academic achievement.

LONG-TERM IMPACT OF TELEVISION ON COGNITIVE DEVELOPMENT AND ACADEMIC ACHIEVEMENT

The major focus of this *Monograph* is on the long-term associations with preschool television viewing. As reviewed above, only a few studies have examined long-term cognitive or academic correlates of early television viewing, and most have failed to distinguish among different types of television content. There is little evidence for overall direct or indirect effects of television on cognitive development and academic achievement, but where effects are found, they are in the direction of television's reducing achievement and reading.

The bulk of the evidence, on the other hand, favors content-based effects. The early learning hypothesis has the strongest support: Viewers of curriculum-based informative television programs consistently show improvements in vocabulary, school readiness, and academic achievement. A smaller amount of research supports a negative association of viewing violence with academic achievement.

The Recontact Study provides two major improvements over prior research. First, our measures of preschool television viewing, based on viewing diaries, are more detailed and validated than those in most prior studies. This allows analysis of outcomes in relation to viewing diet, not just time spent with television. Second, the interval between preschool viewing and measurement of outcomes is longer than in any prior studies of television and academic achievement.

MEASURES

Academic Achievement

Self-Reported Grades

Adolescents were asked to report their typical high school grades in English, math, and science on a 7-point scale: 0 (*Ds and Fs*), 1 (*Cs and Ds*), 2 (*Mostly Cs*), 3 (*Bs and Cs*), 4 (*Mostly Bs*), 5 (*As and Bs*), 6 (*Mostly As*).

Transcript Records

The 491 returned transcripts were coded for grades, subjects taken, and honors, advanced-standing, or college-level classes. Because the grading systems varied across schools, grades were converted to a 13-point scale ranging from A+ to F. For a few schools that used a 100-point scale, numerical grades were converted to letter grades by creating 13 equal intervals between 100 and the highest number defined as "failing" by that school (they were not all the same). The 13-point letter scale was translated to a numerical one (0 = F to 4.33 = A+) before computing grade point averages (GPAs).

Validity of Self-Reported Grades

In Table 9, the self-reported grades for respondents who granted permission to obtain a transcript are compared with those who did not grant permission. The grades of students who did not grant permission were lower.

For the 491 participants whose transcripts were obtained, self-reported grades in English, math, and science were significantly higher than transcript grades, t (490) = 12.77, t (490) = 14.27, and t (477) = 13.41, all ps < .001, for English, math, and science, respectively. The mean differences, on a 4-point scale, were .26, .35, and .37 for English, math, and science, respectively. Although self-reports were inflated, they were substantially correlated with transcript grades, r (491) = .82, r (491) = .79, and r (478) = .74, all ps < .001, for English, math, and science, respectively. Therefore, individual differences in grades were reasonably captured by self-reports.

TABLE 9

MEAN SELF-REPORTED GRADES OF TEENS WHO DID AND DID NOT RETURN
SIGNED TRANSCRIPT RELEASE FORMS

		Kansas		Massachusetts	
	N	Signed release 248	No release form 26	Signed release 248	No release form 48
Grade point average					
English		3.220	2.577***	3.040	2.698***
		(.773)	(.868)	(.671)	(.666)
Math		3.022	2.404***	2.911	2.625*
		(.792)	(.775)	(.778)	(.615)
Science		3.282	2.827**	2.939	2.635**
		(.721)	(.787)	(.727)	(.705)
Overall		3.175	2.603***	2.964	2.653***
		(.641)	(.667)	(.572)	(.521)

Note. The potential range of scores was 0 to 4.33. Significant differences between those who did and did not return a form are indicated by asterisks. Standard deviations are in parentheses.
$*p < .05, **p < .01, ***p < .001$, two-tailed t tests.

Regressions of self-reported grades on transcript records were used to impute grades for the 79 individuals whose transcripts were not received. The transcripts indicated that ninth graders received higher grades than did students in later years in high school. Because the slope and intercept of the regression lines predicting English, math, and science grades differed as a function of grade level and whether or not the teen was still in school, 15 correction equations were used to adjust self-reported grades of participants without transcripts. The 15 equations covered the three subject matter areas for teens in 9th, 10th, 11th, and 12th grades and for those not in school.

Grade Point Averages

The GPAs used in the analyses were those reported in the transcripts for the 491 students with transcripts and the imputed grades from self-reports for the 79 students without transcripts. Separate GPAs in English, math, and science were calculated. The average GPA was the mean of the GPAs in these three academic subjects. The achievement indicators were limited to these three subject matter areas because they are common across most high school curricula and because they are "core" academic achievement domains.

Book Use and Homework

The summary measure of leisure time book reading is described in Chapter 3. Participants were asked how many days per week they did homework and, on these days, the amount of time spent doing homework. Simultaneous use of music, television, and the telephone while doing English, math, and science homework was also measured. The percentages of time that homework was being done while using each of these media were recorded.

Achievement Motivation

The two constructs measured to assess achievement motivation were competence beliefs and subjective task value for English, math, and science. The items were adapted from Eccles (1983). For students no longer in high school, items were phrased in the past tense, referring to high school subjects.

Competence Beliefs

Self-concept of ability was assessed with two items for each subject area: "How good in English/math/science are you? Would you say you are excellent, very good, good, fair, or poor?" and "Compared to all the students in your grade in school, how would you say you rank in English/math/science? Are you better, about the same, or worse?" If the person responded "better" or "worse," the interviewer asked, "Are you a lot better/worse or a little better/worse?" to generate a 5-point unfolding scale: 1 (*a lot worse*), 2 (*a little worse*), 3 (*about the same*), 4 (*a little better*), 5 (*a lot better*). Expectancies of success were measured by asking participants how well they thought they would do in advanced English/math/science courses on a scale from 0 to 100 where 50 was passing. The competence belief items within each domain were transformed to standard z scores with a mean of 0 and a standard deviation of 1 and combined to form a single score for each domain. The average across domains was also computed.

Subjective task value for each subject matter area was assessed with two questions: "In general, how useful is what you learn in English/math/science?" and "Is the amount of effort it will take to do well in English/math/science this year worthwhile to you?" Responses were coded on a 5-point Likert scale ranging from 1 (*not at all useful/worthwhile*) to 5 (*very useful/worthwhile*). Totals for English, math, and science and the average of the three were computed.

Highest Math Class Selected

According to expectancy-value theory, one outcome of achievement motivation is setting a high level of aspiration. In school, students with high motivation are likely to take more-difficult and more-advanced courses than those with lower motivation. Math classes were selected to test this hypothesis because math courses follow a clear sequence; they become increasingly difficult for many students; and students have considerable discretion in choosing advanced math even if they are in a college preparatory program. Comparable measures were not formed for English and science. In English, the content is not arranged sequentially, and most college-bound students expect to take English during their entire high school careers. Although students have some discretion in choosing science courses, most high school science is not sequential. In many high schools it is arbitrary, for example, whether one takes biology, geology, or chemistry first.

Each respondent was asked to name the last math class taken in high school. Those who were still in school were also asked to name the highest-level math class they planned to take. The 185 different math classes mentioned were classified according to difficulty from 0 (e.g., remedial classes such as "Math—Multiplication/Division") to 10 (e.g., "Differential Equations"). Honors classes were coded one level higher than nonhonors versions of the same courses. The score for each adolescent was the highest-level math class to be completed by the time of high school graduation or termination.

RESULTS

Grades

Analyses of variance indicated significant sex and site differences in all three academic subjects as well as on average GPA, $Fs(1,565) > 8.62$, $ps < .01$. Girls and Kansas participants achieved higher grades. The mean overall GPAs were KS males = 2.69 ($SD = .80$), MA males = 2.43 ($SD = .70$), KS females = 3.07 ($SD = .75$), MA females = 2.63 ($SD = .61$). The site difference is probably due to the fact that Kansas participants were younger than those in Massachusetts; grades were higher for younger teens. Although correlations among grades across academic subjects ranged from .60 to .71, we examined the relations to television viewing for each subject separately as well as for average GPA because the theories of television effects make some differential predictions.

Relations of Viewing to Grades

As described in Chapter 2, we examined the associations between television viewing and high school grades with hierarchical multiple regression analysis. Background variables were parents' education, birth order, sex, site, and the sex-by-site interaction. We did not include PPVT-R scores as a control for preschool intellectual functioning because prior research indicated that child informative viewing before the age of 5 predicts 5-year-old PPVT-R scores (Rice et al., 1990). Hence, controlling for it might remove some of the effects of early viewing.

In one model, total television time in preschool and adolescent years was tested. In other models, we tested single program categories separately, as well as viewing diet (informative, violent, other) in early childhood and adolescence. In all cases the simple and more complex models provided consistent conclusions, both with and without outliers included in the analyses (see Chapter 2 for the identification and treatment of outliers). The results presented here are based on the most complete models that include viewing diet in preschool and adolescence. The tables and text presentation of standardized betas exclude outliers. All the analyses predicting grades indicated significant interactions with sex; consequently, separate analyses were done for males and females.

Overall Viewing Times

First let us consider the results for total viewing, shown in Table 10. Boys' preschool total time spent with television was positively associated with high school GPA averaged across English, math, and science, but the association was negative for girls. Teen total viewing, on the other hand, was not significantly associated with high school grades for either sex. When English, math, and science were considered separately, preschool viewing was positively related to grades in each subject for boys. For girls the negative relation was significant for science, marginal for English, and not significant for math.

The theories that hypothesize a general deleterious effect of the television medium (i.e., time displacement, attention deficit, language deficit, entertainment and mental effort) seemingly receive support from the negative association with grades for girls, but the positive association for boys clearly contradicts these predictions. The lack of association of grades with teen viewing, moreover, is damaging to the displacement hypothesis.

The analyses do not support theories that predict effects of overall viewing on specific academic subjects. According to the language deficit hypothesis, television viewing should be particularly damaging to

TABLE 10

SUMMARY OF REGRESSION ANALYSES PREDICTING HIGH SCHOOL GRADES
FROM TOTAL PRESCHOOL AND TEEN TELEVISION VIEWING

	Grade point average							
	Total		English		Math		Science	
	Male[a]	Female[b]	Male[a]	Female[c]	Male[a]	Female[a]	Male[a]	Female[a]
Background								
Site (MA)	−.13*	−.30***	−.11*	−.27***	−.08	−.21**	−.15*	−.33***
Parent education	.34***	.18**	.35***	.19**	.26***	.15*	.32***	.16**
Birth order	−.05	−.17**	−.05	−.19**	−.05	−.12*	−.02	−.12*
Television								
Preschool total	.16**	−.15**	.14*	−.11‡	.13*	−.09	.15*	−.15*
Teen total	−.06	−.06	−.07	−.07	−.02	−.05	−.08	−.03
Adjusted R^2	.143***	.197***	.141***	.182***	.076***	.098***	.128***	.175***

Note. Dependent variables are GPAs scaled 0 to 4.33. Entries are standardized regression coefficients and adjusted R^2 values.
[a]no outliers; [b]excluding 1 outlier; [c]excluding 2 outliers.
‡p = .073. *p < .05. **p < .01. ***p < .001.

achievement in the most language-oriented subject, English. English grades were positively predicted by overall preschool viewing in boys, and the negative relation was marginal for girls. The entertainment and mental effort hypothesis predicts that the negative effects should be particularly manifested in math grades. Preschool viewing was positively associated with math grades for boys and not significantly associated for girls.

Viewing Diet

We broke down total viewing into the content categories informative, violent, and all other programming in preschool and adolescent viewing. For boys, preschool viewing of child informative programs was positively associated with high school grades in all subjects (see Table 11). Preschool violence viewing by boys was unrelated to high school grades, but teen violence viewing was negatively associated with grades in English, grades in science, and average grades.

For girls, preschool child informative viewing did not significantly predict high school grades, although the associations were positive. When girls' preschool viewing was considered without including teen viewing as a mediator, preschool violence viewing was negatively associated with high school grades. When teen viewing was considered for girls, however, teen violence viewing interacted with site. Separate analyses for each site indicated that preschool violence viewing was negatively associated with grades for Kansas girls, but not for Massachusetts girls. For Massachusetts girls, on the other hand, there were negative relations of teen violence viewing

TABLE 11

Summary of Regression Analyses Predicting High School Grades
From Preschool and Teen Categories of Television Viewing

| | Grade point average | | | | | | | |
| | Total | | English | | Math | | Science | |
	Male[a]	Female[a]	Male[a]	Female[b]	Male[a]	Female[a]	Male[a]	Female[a]
Background								
Parent education	.29***	.17**	.31***	.19**	.22***	.15*	.27***	.14*
Birth order	−.02	−.13*	−.02	−.16**	−.04	−.09	.01	−.08
Site (MA)	−.16**	−.37	−.13*	−.07	−.12‡	−.46	−.18**	−.36
Preschool TV								
Informative	.21***	.05	.19**	.02	.17**	.03	.22***	.09
Violent	.03	−.19**	.10	−.14*	−.04	−.21**	.01	−.17*
Other	.03	.00	−.03	.00	.06	.10	.06	−.05
Teen TV								
Informative	.04	.08	−.04	.08	.07	.07	.08	.08
Violent	−.12*	.01	−.11*	.00	−.08	−.01	−.13*	.02
Other	−.10‡	−.06	−.07	−.10‡	−.04	−.03	−.17**	−.04
Interactions								
Site × Teen Violent	—	.48**	—	.37*	—	.39*	—	.46**
Adjusted R^2	.180***	.223***	.173***	.188***	.092***	.120***	.190***	.199***

Note. Entries are standardized regression coefficients and adjusted R^2 values.
[a]no outliers; [b]excluding 2 outliers.
‡$p < .10$. *$p < .05$. **$p < .01$. ***$p < .001$.

with grades (see Table 12). Average GPAs as a function of quartiles of child informative viewing are shown in Figure 1, and means by quartiles of violence viewing appear in Figure 2.

The results are largely in accord with the content-based theories insofar as preschool child informative viewing was positively related to academic success in high school and violence viewing was negatively related to academic success, but the results were qualified by different patterns for males and females. Neither early learning theory nor violence viewing theory predicts different effects of viewing for males and females.

The viewing diet results clarify the sex differences found for overall viewing. The positive relations of preschool television viewing for boys are clearly due to child informative content, and the negative relations of preschool television viewing for girls are largely due to violent content. The content of programs children viewed as preschoolers appears to be more relevant in predicting high school grades than how much they watched television in general.

Specific Child Informative Programs

Sesame Street is the focus of some of the theories concerning the effects of television on academic achievement. In contrast to the early learning

51

TABLE 12

Summary of Regression Analyses Predicting High School Grades From Preschool
and Teen Categories of Television Viewing for Females Split by Site

| | Grade point average | | | | | | | |
| | Total | | English | | Math | | Science | |
	KS[a]	MA[a]	KS[b]	MA[a]	KS[a]	MA[a]	KS[a]	MA[a]
Background								
Parent education	.17‡	.22*	.18*	.21*	.11	.20*	.14	.17‡
Birth order	−.17*	−.06	−.25**	−.09	−.11	−.08	−.15‡	.00
Preschool TV								
Informative	.08	.05	.05	.04	.05	.01	.09	.08
Violent	−.28**	−.10	−.20‡	−.07	−.29*	−.11	−.27*	−.07
Other	.01	.00	−.07	−.02	.10	.09	−.02	−.08
Teen TV								
Informative	.09	.10	.14‡	.05	.04	.10	.06	.12
Violent	.13	−.22**	.12	−.17*	.10	−.20*	.15‡	−.20*
Other	−.13	.03	−.11	−.08	−.14	.09	−.11	.04
Adjusted R^2	.165***	.077*	.184***	.065*	.076*	.058*	.141***	.053*

Note. Entries are standardized regression coefficients and adjusted R^2 values.
[a]no outliers; [b]excluding 1 outlier.
‡$p < .10$. *$p < .05$. **$p < .01$. ***$p < .001$.

theory prediction of a positive impact of *Sesame Street* viewing, Healy's (1990) language hypothesis and J. L. Singer's (1980) attention-deficit hypotheses predict a negative impact. Similarly, according to some, the entertainment and mental effort hypothesis would predict a negative impact of *Sesame Street* (Healy, 1990; Moody, 1980; Winn, 1977). We therefore did a separate analysis of *Sesame Street* viewing in relation to high school grades using hierarchical regression to predict grades. The television predictors were hours of *Sesame Street* at age 5 and hours of all other child informative viewing not including *Sesame Street*. These analyses did not include teen viewing, as there is no obvious teen viewing diet analog of *Sesame Street* that would mediate the relations. Results are shown in Table 13.

The most straightforward results concern math and science grades, for which there were no significant interactions with sex or site. There was a significant and positive association between *Sesame Street* viewing and science grades, and the association with math grades was positive but only marginally significant ($p = .056$). For both average and English grades, there were significant interactions of *Sesame Street* viewing with sex. In separate analyses for males and females, there were significant positive associations for boys but not for girls. Surprisingly, viewing child informative programs other than *Sesame Street* did not significantly predict grades. The positive relation of child informative viewing to high school grades

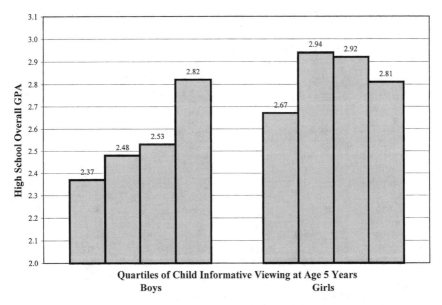

FIGURE 1.—High school GPA by quartiles of child informative viewing at age 5

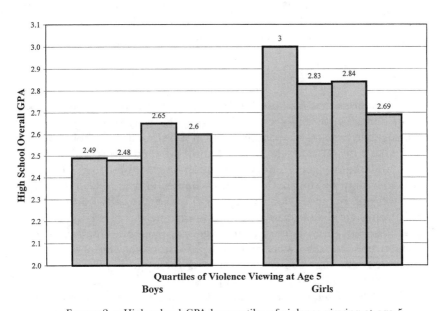

FIGURE 2.—High school GPA by quartiles of violence viewing at age 5

TABLE 13

SUMMARY OF REGRESSION ANALYSES PREDICTING HIGH SCHOOL GRADES
FROM PRESCHOOL *SESAME STREET* VIEWING

	Grade point average					
	Total		English		Math[a]	Science[b]
	Male[a]	Female[b]	Male[a]	Female[a]	Both sexes	Both sexes
Background						
Parent education	.30***	.22***	.32***	.23***	.20***	.24***
Birth order	−.01	−.13*	−.02	−.18**	−.07	−.04
Sex (female)	—	—	—	—	.122**	.175**
Site (MA)	−.16**	−.23***	−.13*	−.22**	−.14**	−.20***
Sex × Site	—	—	—	—	−.04	−.06
Preschool TV						
Sesame Street	.18**	.09	.19**	.06	.09‡	.16***
Other informative	.09	−.10	.05	−.09	.00	−.01
Adjusted R^2	.186***	.185***	.181***	.183***	.108***	.187***

Note. Entries are standardized regression coefficients and adjusted R^2 values.
[a]no outliers; [b]excluding 1 outlier.
‡$p < .10$. *$p < .05$. **$p < .01$. ***$p < .001$.

therefore appeared to be primarily due to *Sesame Street* viewing. Contrary to the language hypothesis, the attention-deficit hypothesis, and the entertainment and mental effort hypothesis, *Sesame Street* viewing was associated with positive long-term academic outcomes.

Book Use

The theories that hypothesize deleterious effects of the television medium predict that overall preschool television viewing should have a long-term negative impact on reading books not assigned for school. Because books take time to read, require a knowledge and appreciation of language, and require some effort and sustained attention to read and decode, television viewing both as a preschooler and as a teen should be associated with reduced book reading. In contrast, the early learning theory predicts that child informative programming such as *Sesame Street* fosters literacy and an appreciation of language; consequently, there should be increased book reading associated with preschool viewing of child informative programming. The violence viewing theory makes no obvious predictions with respect to book reading, because the negative effects of violence are considered to be primarily social and behavioral, not cognitive. Consequently, we did not separately consider the relation of violence viewing to book reading. The simple relations of violence viewing and book reading (see Chapter 3) indicate that teen violence viewing is positively related to book reading.

The correlations of book use with grades were .20, .11, .21, and .19 with English, math, science, and average GPA, respectively. Five-year-old total viewing *positively* predicted later book use, β = .327, p < .001, adjusted R^2 = .137, p < .001, and there were no sex differences in the slope relating early television viewing to teen book use. When we included teen hours of viewing, there was a significant interaction of teen viewing by both site and sex (see Table 14). Separate analyses of each site and sex showed positive relations between preschool hours of viewing and book use for all subgroups, but teen viewing predicted book use only for the Massachusetts females. Importantly, the relation between preschool television use and leisure reading was uniformly positive and not mediated by teen television time. These results run contrary to all the theories predicting negative associations between preschool or teen television viewing and book use.

When we considered viewing diet by comparing child informative with all other viewing, a readily interpretable pattern emerged. Five-year-old child informative viewing was positively associated with teen book use, whereas all other viewing was not. The results are shown in Table 15. A plot of book use as a function of child informative viewing appears in Figure 3. Children in the top quartile of child informative viewing were about half a standard deviation above the mean, and those in the bottom quartile were about half a standard deviation below the mean. The analyses

TABLE 14

SUMMARY OF REGRESSION ANALYSES PREDICTING BOOK USE FROM TOTAL PRESCHOOL AND TEEN VIEWING

	Male		Female	
	KS[a]	MA[b]	KS[a]	MA[b]
Background				
Parent education	.19*	.30***	.09	.13
Birth order	−.17*	−.17*	−.06	−.09
Television				
Preschool total	.33***	.33***	.22*	.31***
Teen total	.05	−.06	−.07	.18*
Adjusted R^2	.138***	.200***	.015	.151***

Note. Entries are standardized regression coefficients and adjusted R^2 values.
[a]no outliers; [b]excluding 1 outlier.
*p < .05. **p < .01. ***p < .001.

TABLE 15

SUMMARY OF REGRESSION ANALYSES PREDICTING TEEN BOOK USE FROM PRESCHOOL
AND TEEN INFORMATIVE AND ENTERTAINMENT TELEVISION

	Both sites[b]	Kansas[a]	Massachusetts[b]
Background			
Parent education	.08*	.09	.11*
Birth order	−.03	.03	.01
Sex (female)	.10	.10‡	.07
Site (MA)	.23*	—	—
Sex × Site	−.02	—	—
Preschool TV			
Informative	.59***	.50***	.65***
Other	−.03	−.02	−.07
Teen TV			
Informative	.01	.10‡	−.07
Other	−.11**	−.12*	−.09*
Interactions			
Site × Teen Other	.22*	—	—
Adjusted R^2	.369***	.282***	.440***

Note. Entries are standardized regression coefficients and adjusted R^2 values.
[a]excluding 1 outlier; [b]excluding 2 outliers.
*$p < .05$. ***$p < .001$.

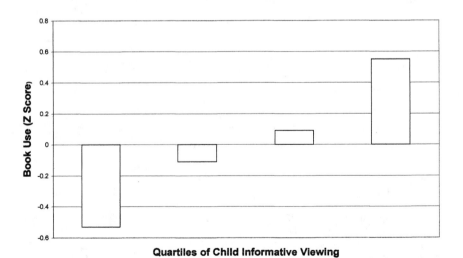

Quartiles of Child Informative Viewing

FIGURE 3.—Teen book use (composite measure) by quartiles of child informative viewing at age 5

incorporating preschool viewing diet accounted for considerably more of the variance, 34.9%, than that accounted for by total preschool viewing time, 13.7%.

When teen viewing diet was included, child informative viewing still strongly predicted teen book use. Teen viewing of entertainment programming, however, was negatively associated with book use (see Table 15). Teen viewing of adult informative programming was positively associated with book use only for Kansas participants. Taken together the results indicated a relatively strong positive association of 5-year-old viewing of child informative programs with teen book use and a negative association of teen entertainment viewing with book use.

We examined the relation of 5-year-old *Sesame Street* viewing to teen book use because Healy (1990) specifically hypothesized that *Sesame Street* viewing produces an inattention to language, reduced reading ability, and a reduced interest in reading. Following the strategy outlined above, we regressed book use on the background variables and *Sesame Street* viewing as well as all other child informative viewing not including *Sesame Street*. Although there was a significant positive relation of *Sesame Street* viewing to teen book use, a significant interaction of other child informative viewing with sex necessitated separate analyses for males and females (see Table 16).

Sesame Street viewing was positively associated with teen book use for both males and females, clearly contradicting the language deficit hypothesis. The interaction of other child informative viewing with sex occurred because viewing other child informative programs was also positively related to boys' book use, whereas the relation for girls was negative.

TABLE 16

SUMMARY OF REGRESSION ANALYSES PREDICTING TEEN BOOK USE FROM PRESCHOOL *SESAME STREET* AND OTHER CHILD INFORMATIVE TELEVISION

	Male[a]	Female[b]
Background		
Parent education	.28***	.20***
Birth order	.01	−.11‡
Site (MA)	−.19***	−.23***
Preschool TV		
Sesame Street	.16**	.17*
Other informative	.12‡	−.15*
Adjusted R^2	.159***	.183***

Note. Entries are standardized regression coefficients and adjusted R^2 values.
[a]No outliers; [b]excluding 1 outlier.
‡$p < .10$. *$p < .05$. ***$p < .001$.

Homework

Success in high school requires diligent completion of homework assignments. We asked the participants how much time in a typical week they spent on homework. An analysis of variance indicated that females spent more time on homework than males, $F(1,566) = 39.53$, $p < .001$; that Massachusetts participants spent more time on homework than Kansas participants, $F(1,566) = 12.34$, $p < .001$; and an interaction, $F(1,566) = 5.81$, $p < .05$, due to a larger sex difference for Massachusetts participants than for those in Kansas: 5.61 and 9.60 hr for Massachusetts boys and girls, as compared with 5.10 and 6.88 hr for Kansas boys and girls, respectively.

Time spent on homework was positively related to grades. In a regression analysis predicting average grades from time spent on homework, with controls for individual and family variables, time on homework was a significant predictor; $\beta = .185$, $p < .001$, and the adjusted $R^2 = .200$, $p < .001$.

Displacement theory predicts that time spent with television as a teen should be negatively associated with time spent on homework. That theory was not supported. The simple correlation between teen television viewing time and homework time in the total sample was −.02. In the four combinations of site and sex the correlations ranged from −.08 for Kansas males to .10 for Massachusetts females. None of the correlations was statistically significant.

Some teens do homework with television; for these teens, homework time could be positively related to television time. We asked the participants what percentage of time they did homework with television for English, math, and science assignments. Overall, 28.3% of participants reported ever doing homework with television. Analyses predicting high school grades as a function of whether or not homework is done with television yielded no relations of interest.

Motivation for Academic Achievement

Relations Among Motivational Constructs and Grades

Competence beliefs were more highly correlated with grades than were subjective task values. The correlations of competence beliefs with GPA were average = .61, English = .56, math = .63, science = .49; those for subjective task value and GPA were average = .23, English = .19, math = .21, science = .18. The highest math course was related to GPA, $r = .56$. All correlations were significant at $p < .01$.

Competence Beliefs

Because the hypotheses guiding the analyses did not lead to specific predictions about the relations of total television viewing to achievement motivation, and because the analyses of grades did not support a consistent relation of total television to achievement, we present the viewing diet analyses only for competence beliefs and incentive value. There were no significant interactions of viewing with sex except on English competence beliefs. Therefore, hierarchical regressions predicting average, math, and science competence beliefs are presented in Table 17 for the total sample. Results for males' and females' English competence beliefs appear in Table 18. It seemed likely that relations of viewing to achievement motivation could be mediated by grades: Teens with good grades are likely to perceive themselves as more competent than those with poor grades. Therefore, a second regression model that included GPA was tested for each achievement motivation outcome. The results are shown in Tables 17 and 18.

Child informative viewing was a consistent predictor of average competence beliefs and of competence beliefs in each of the three domains.

TABLE 17

SUMMARY OF REGRESSION ANALYSES PREDICTING AVERAGE, MATH, AND SCIENCE COMPETENCE BELIEFS FROM PRESCHOOL AND TEEN CATEGORIES OF TELEVISION VIEWING

| | Competence beliefs | | | | | |
| | Average | | Math | | Science | |
	Model 1	Model 2	Model 1	Model 2	Model 1	Model 2
Background						
Parent education	.25***	.11**	.13**	.01	.17***	.07‡
Birth order	−.07*	−.04	−.01	.03	−.09*	−.07‡
Sex (female)	−.04	−.15***	−.09*	−.16***	−.11*	−.18***
Site (MA)	.03	.11**	−.03	−.15***	.10*	−.01
Sex × Site	−.02	.01	−.02	.01	.06	.02
GPA	—	.62***	—	.68***	—	.49**
Preschool TV						
Child informative	.13**	.04	.09*	.02	.09*	.02
Violent	.00	.02	.02	.08*	−.04	−.03
Other	−.06	−.05	−.06	−.10*	.00	.03
Teen TV						
Informative	.07‡	.03	.06	.01	.05	.01
Violent	−.03	.04	−.07‡	−.01	.03	.08*
Other	−.11*	−.09**	−.02	−.01	−.11**	−.10*
Adjusted R^2	.121***	.429***	.031**	.438***	.084***	.285***

Note. Entries are standardized regression coefficients and adjusted R^2 values.
‡$p < .10$. *$p < .05$. **$p < .01$. ***$p < .001$.

TABLE 18

SUMMARY OF REGRESSION ANALYSES PREDICTING ENGLISH COMPETENCE BELIEFS FROM
PRESCHOOL AND TEEN CATEGORIES OF TELEVISION VIEWING FOR MALES AND FEMALES

	Model 1		Model 2	
	Male	Female	Male	Female
Background				
Parent education	.29***	.27***	.14*	.18***
Birth order	−.06	−.08	.06	.00
Site (MA)	.02	−.03	−.08	−.15**
GPA	—	—	.53***	.49***
Preschool TV				
Informative	.15**	.07	.04	.06
Violent	−.03	.06	−.10	.11‡
Other	−.05	−.11‡	.01	−.09
Teen TV				
Informative	−.02	.10‡	.00	.06
Violent	−.03	.06	.03	.10*
Other	−.01	−.25***	.03	−.22***
Adjusted R^2	.119**	.171***	.352***	.368***

Note. Entries are standardized regression coefficients and adjusted R^2 values. Model 1 contains controls for background variables. Model 2 adds GPA as a control.

‡$p < .10$. *$p < .05$. **$p < .01$. ***$p < .001$.

For English competency, these relations were stronger for boys than for girls. For all competence belief measures, the relations of child informative viewing were reduced to nonsignificant levels when GPA was entered, suggesting that the relations of child informative viewing to competence beliefs were mediated by academic performance.

There were some positive relations between viewing violent programs in the preschool or teen years and competence beliefs once GPA was controlled (but not without GPA as a control). The direction was contrary to prediction. For girls, with grades controlled, preschool and teen exposure to violence were positively related to English competence beliefs. For both sexes combined, preschool exposure to violent content was a positive predictor of math beliefs, and teen exposure predicted science competence beliefs. That is, when students were statistically equated for academic achievement, there was some tendency for those who watched more cartoons and action-adventure programs (relative to other types of television) to evaluate their competence more favorably than did students whose diets included less violence or to overestimate their competence.

By contrast, students whose diets contained relatively high exposure to "other" programming, particularly in the teen years, had lower average competence beliefs and lower beliefs in their competence in English and science than did students whose diets contained relatively little "other" programming. Much of the programming included in this category is general entertainment fare (e.g., situation comedies, talk, variety, soap operas). For English competency, this pattern was especially pronounced for girls. The negative relation of viewing "other" programs to competence beliefs remained in most cases even when GPA was controlled.

Subjective Task Values

Adolescents' averaged subjective task values and values for the three academic subjects (English, math, and science) were regressed on viewing using the same models as those used for competence beliefs. The interactions of Sex × Child Informative Viewing were significant in most analyses, and the interactions of sex with other viewing categories were also sometimes significant. Therefore, analyses were performed separately for males and females. The results for averaged task value are shown in Table 19, and those for math and science are shown in Table 20. None of the relations of viewing to task value in English were significant, so the analyses are not shown.

TABLE 19

SUMMARY OF REGRESSION ANALYSES PREDICTING AVERAGE SUBJECTIVE TASK VALUES FROM PRESCHOOL AND TEEN CATEGORIES OF TELEVISION VIEWING FOR MALES AND FEMALES

	Model 1		Model 2	
	Male	Female	Male	Female
Background				
Parent education	−.02	.07	−.05	.03
Birth order	−.07	−.12‡	−.07	−.09
Site (MA)	.13‡	.10	.11‡	.03
GPA	—	—	.10	.22***
Preschool TV				
Informative	.14*	−.03	.12‡	−.04
Violent	.01	−.03	.00	.00
Other	.04	.10	.04	.10
Teen TV				
Informative	.09	.00	.09	−.02
Violent	.03	−.07	.04	−.05
Other	−.02	−.12‡	−.02	−.11‡
Adjusted R^2	.038*	.034*	.044*	.071**

Note. Entries are standardized regression coefficients and adjusted R^2 values. Model 1 contains controls for background variables. Model 2 adds GPA as a control.

‡$p < .10$. *$p < .05$. **$p < .01$. ***$p < .001$.

TABLE 20

Summary of Regression Analyses Predicting Subjective Task Values in Math and Science From Preschool and Teen Categories of Television Viewing for Males and Females

	Math				Science			
	Model 1		Model 2		Model 1		Model 2	
	Male	Female	Male	Female	Male	Female	Male	Female
Background								
Parent education	−.11‡	−.01	−.14*	−.04	.06	.13*	.04	.11‡
Birth order	−.06	−.14*	−.06	−.13*	−.09	−.02	−.08	−.01
Site (MA)	.16*	.12‡	.15*	.07	.09	.06	.08	.02
GPA	—	—	.15*	.20**	—	—	.08	.17*
Preschool TV								
Informative	.12*	−.02	.10	−.03	.14*	.02	.12‡	.02
Violent	−.02	.01	−.02	.04	−.04	−.12‡	−.06	−.09
Other	.08	.12‡	.08	.11	.05	.13‡	.05	.14‡
Teen TV								
Informative	.07	−.03	.05	−.04	.03	.05	.02	.04
Violent	.05	−.14*	.06	−.12*	.10‡	.05	.11‡	.06
Other	.07	−.06	.07	−.06	−.11‡	−.09	−.12‡	−.07
Adjusted R^2	.060*	.048**	.076***	.081***	.045*	.024‡	.044*	.044*

Note. Entries are standardized regression coefficients and adjusted R^2 values. Model 1 contains controls for background variables. Model 2 adds GPA as a control.

‡$p < .10$. *$p < .05$. **$p < .01$. ***$p < .001$.

Viewing child informative programs was significantly and positively related to average subjective task value of high school subject matter and to the value attached to math and science for males, but not for females. The relation of child informative viewing to males' average subjective task value and to value for science remained at a borderline level of significance when GPA was included, suggesting that the relations were not mediated entirely by academic achievement.

Viewing violence in preschool was not related to subjective task values in any subject area, but teen viewing of violence was negatively related to math value for females and tended to be positively related to science value for males.

For girls, the amount of time spent viewing other entertainment programming in preschool was marginally *positively* related to task values of math and science. In adolescence, however, the pattern was reversed. Girls whose television diets were relatively high in other entertainment programs tended to have lower average task values and lower values for math than did other girls. For boys, there was a borderline tendency for the same pattern to occur for science.

Course Choices: Highest Math Class Taken or Planned

Analyses of the score representing the difficulty level of the highest math class taken or planned were conducted to test the direct relation of viewing to course choice (Model 1; see Table 21). High school grades were then added as a mediator (Model 2). Then competence beliefs and subjective task values were added to test whether they mediated the relation (Model 3). In all of the models, controlling for background variables, the interactions of child informative viewing with sex were significant. Therefore, we conducted analyses separately for each sex; they appear in Table 21. In all of the models tested, child informative viewing was significantly and positively related to choosing high-level math classes for males but not for females. None of the other viewing categories predicted the level of math courses. Child informative viewing was a predictor of boys' math course choices even when math GPA was included in the model, suggesting that the relations of viewing were not mediated entirely by academic performance.

TABLE 21

SUMMARY OF REGRESSION ANALYSES PREDICTING HIGHEST MATH CLASS TAKEN OR PLANNED FROM PRESCHOOL AND TEEN CATEGORIES OF TELEVISION VIEWING FOR MALES AND FEMALES

	Model 1		Model 2		Model 3	
	Male	Female	Male	Female	Male	Female
Background						
Parent education	.29***	.18**	.20***	.11‡	.20***	.12*
Birth order	−.05	−.13*	−.03	−.09‡	−.04	−.09‡
Site (MA)	.02	.01	−.03	−.10‡	−.01	−.06
GPA	—	—	.47***	.47***	.27***	.23**
Competence belief math	—	—	—	—	.28***	.33***
Value math	—	—	—	—	.08‡	.09‡
Preschool TV						
Informative	.21*	.00	.14**	−.02	.13**	−.04
Violent	.08	−.03	.10	.05	.07	.02
Other	−.03	−.05	−.05	−.08	−.01	−.08
Teen TV						
Informative	−.01	.04	−.04	−.02	−.06	−.02
Violent	.03	−.08	.00	.03	−.02	.00
Other	.03	−.06	−.04	−.05	−.04	−.03
Adjusted R^2	.135***	.049**	.333***	.244***	.381***	.324***

Note. Entries are standardized regression coefficients and adjusted R^2 values. Model 1 contains controls for background variables. Model 2 adds GPA as a control. Model 3 adds competence belief and value for math.
‡$p < .10$. *$p < .05$. **$p < .01$. ***$p < .001$.

In a final model, competence beliefs and task value for math were added to the prediction equation. These two constructs increased the variance explained by 4.8% for boys and 8% for girls, but child informative viewing was still significant for boys. The contribution of GPA was reduced. In fact, competence beliefs about math accounted for more variance than did math GPA. These analyses suggest that competence beliefs and, to a slight degree, subjective task value for math mediate some of the relation between GPA and choosing advanced math courses. None of these constructs fully explained the positive relation of child informative viewing to taking higher level math courses.

CONCLUSIONS

The findings are consistent with content-based theories and provide little support for hypotheses about effects of the medium arising from time displacement or formal features of programs. Our finding that boys' viewing of child informative programs at age 5 positively predicted high school grades in English, math, and science supports the early learning theory. Although the associations for girls were positive, they were not statistically significant. The most academically oriented of the age-appropriate child informative programs was *Sesame Street,* which constituted 54% of all the child informative viewing by our participants. *Sesame Street* viewing was positively related to English grades for boys, was marginally positive with respect to math grades for both sexes, and was positively related to science grades for both sexes.

These long-term relations between viewing educational programming in the preschool years and high school achievement appeared with controls for family characteristics, particularly parent education, that are typically strong predictors of both achievement and viewing. They also occurred with controls for other categories of preschool viewing and for all categories of adolescent viewing.

The violence viewing theory received some support insofar as girls who were heavy viewers of violent programs (primarily cartoons) at age 5 had lower high school grades in English, math, and science than did those who watched less violence. Some of these associations were, however, mediated by teen viewing of violence. Although there was no significant relation of preschool violence viewing to boys' grades, teen violence viewing predicted lower grades.

By contrast, there was little support for the time-displacement theory. Although girls' preschool time with television was negatively associated with high school grades, the association was positive for boys. Both patterns were explained by program content. Similarly, the results contradicted the predictions, based on formal features of television, that viewing television, particularly *Sesame Street*, would lead to attention deficits (J. L. Singer, 1980), to language deficits (Healy, 1990), or to low levels of mental effort (e.g., Koolstra & van der Voort, 1996) and consequently to reduced high school grades or leisure reading. Instead, *Sesame Street* viewing was positively related to high school grades and to teen book use.

The results are consistent with the idea that informative and educational content of television in the early years leads to later academic achievement but do not identify the possible pathways of influence. One possibility is that the positive relation between child informative viewing and academic achievement is mediated by early cognitive achievement. We recalculated the regressions predicting high school grades and book use, adding PPVT-R standard scores as a potential mediating variable. We pointed out earlier that PPVT-R at age 5 may have included some of the effects of earlier child informative viewing, so it was not an appropriate control variable. It is a reasonable index of cognitive achievement at age 5, however. If television still predicts later achievement after controlling for PPVT-R, then the case is strengthened that the effects of early television viewing are at least partly social and/or motivational and are not mediated solely by early achievement. When PPVT-R standard score was introduced as a background variable, none of the regression results changed substantially, although PPVT-R was itself frequently a significant positive predictor. These results suggest that the relations of early childhood informative viewing to long-term achievement are not due to basic intellectual competence or early cognitive learning alone.

The relations of early educational viewing to leisure reading, competence beliefs, and value for achievement suggest that such viewing could also have contributed to children's interest and motivation in academic pursuits. Child informative viewing was a strong predictor of teen book reading. Although academic achievement probably mediated the relations of child informative viewing to students' beliefs about their own competence, viewing made independent contributions to subjective task value and selection of high-level math courses, at least for males. It is possible that viewing children's educational programming stimulates children's interest in science and math or conveys messages about the importance of these topics in many facets of everyday life.

SUMMARY

The relations between early television viewing and later academic achievement and book use appear to be due more ·to what the child watches on television than to how much time the child spends watching television. Although total time with television in preschool was positively related to grades for boys, the effect was due entirely to child informative programs, especially *Sesame Street*. Viewing *Sesame Street* was also associated with higher grades in math and science for girls, but watching violent programs at age 5 years was a negative predictor of high school grades for girls. Preschool viewing of child informative programs, especially *Sesame Street*, was associated with high levels of leisure time book use for both males and females, and it predicted the value attached to achievement and the level of math classes selected for boys, even when high school grades were controlled.

V. CREATIVITY

Creativity is often defined as cognitive fluency and originality, but it may also be manifested in products and activities in the "creative" arts or by fantasy and imagination. Although anyone with normal cognitive abilities is capable of being creative (Amabile, 1983), creative thought requires appropriate stimulation, intrinsic motivation, and reinforcement of efforts (Sternberg & Lubart, 1991). It is generally accepted that environmental influences in early childhood can substantially affect later creative achievement (see Mumford & Gustafson, 1988, for a review). Accordingly, exposure to television may influence children's creativity. Contradictory hypotheses about the influence of television on creative thinking, drawn from the theories discussed in Chapter 1, roughly parallel those for television's influence on cognitive development and academic achievement (for an extensive review of these theories with respect to creativity, see Valkenburg & van der Voort, 1994).

HYPOTHESES BASED ON CONTENT

Early Learning

According to Gardner (1982), television can stimulate children's creativity by providing ideas to draw upon during creative tasks. Some television programs have been specifically designed to enable children "to discover and to use their creativity and imagination" (Hamgarth & Reus, 1991, p. 4). A content analysis of educational programs indicates that they frequently contain approaches to creativity (Neapolitan & Huston, 1994).

In early experimental studies, viewing *Mister Rogers' Neighborhood*, which emphasizes imagination and clearly defines boundaries between real and pretend, led to increased observed persistence in play activities (Friedrich & Stein, 1973) and fantasy play (Friedrich-Cofer, Huston-Stein, Kipnis, Susman, & Clewett, 1979; D. Singer & Singer, 1990; Tower, Singer, Singer, & Biggs, 1979). Although fantasy play is not identical to creative fluency (Valkenburg & van der Voort, 1994), one may generalize to the other. In evaluations of *Allegra's Window* and *Gullah Gullah Island*, programs designed to promote flexible and creative approaches to social and cognitive problem solving, parents and other caretakers rated viewers as more creative than nonviewers (Bryant & Williams, 1997).

Violence

A second hypothesis suggests that the arousing quality of violent programs fosters aggressive fantasies, restlessness, and impulsivity, which disrupt creativity (J. L. Singer, Singer, & Rapaczynski, 1984). There is also some support for this hypothesis (Valkenburg & van der Voort, 1995). For example, in their longitudinal studies, the Singers have found negative associations between the amount of violence viewed by young children and their amount of imaginative play (J. L. Singer et al., 1984).

HYPOTHESES BASED ON TELEVISION AS A MEDIUM

The more common view is that television as a medium reduces creativity. Four mechanisms have been proposed on the basis of theories presented in Chapter 1. According to the displacement hypothesis, television (regardless of content) takes time away from such activities as reading and active play that are valuable in fostering creativity (L. F. Harrison & T. M. Williams, 1986; Koolstra & van der Voort, 1996; Valkenburg & van der Voort, 1994). According to the rapid pacing hypothesis, television viewers are confronted with images that must be quickly processed in rapid succession, allowing little time for reflection and generative cognitive activity (Greenfield, 1984; J. L. Singer & Singer, 1981; Valkenburg & van der Voort, 1994). According to the visualization hypothesis, the visual nature of television makes it less likely that the viewer will generate novel images (e.g., Greenfield, 1984). Proponents of the passivity hypothesis argue that television provides prepackaged fantasies that require little mental effort, leading to passive intellectual processing rather than to active forms of learning (Salomon, 1984). Because children may be more mentally active when watching child informative television than during entertainment programs (cf. Anderson & Lorch, 1983; Huston & Wright, 1983, 1989), we consider it plausible that the passivity may be a consequence of programming with low intellectual and imaginative demands but not of informative programming that is age-appropriate.

REVIEW OF EARLIER RESEARCH

The theories proposing a general impact of television lead to the prediction that viewing television, regardless of content, will be negatively associated with creativity. Existing studies are sparse and hardly definitive, but the preponderance of evidence supports this prediction, at least under some circumstances (see Valkenburg & van der Voort, 1994, for a review).

Divergent Thinking

In a classic study of the introduction of television (L. F. Harrison & Williams, 1986), the authors compared children from three Canadian towns: one without television, one with one television channel, and one with multiple channels. Children without television had higher verbal ideational fluency scores than children from the towns that had television. After the introduction of television, however, their fluency scores fell to the level of children in the towns that previously had television. These patterns did not emerge for a visual measure of divergent thinking.

Five cross-sectional correlational studies also provide modest support for a relation of television viewing to low levels of divergent thinking (Childs, 1979; Furu, 1971; Peterson, Peterson, & Caroll, 1987; Vogler, 1975; Wade, 1971). After controlling for other variables that could be related to both viewing and creativity, these studies report negative relations between viewing and approximately half of the divergent thinking measures.

In one study of highly gifted children, no relation of program type to creativity was found (Stern, 1973). Children were asked to increase their viewing of one of six program types (e.g., sports or educational programs) for 3 weeks, but there was no check on whether the participants actually watched more of the assigned type of television program. In addition, the creativity of gifted children may be less susceptible to change (especially in an upward direction) than that of typical children.

Creative Imagination

Creativity by young children may be manifested most obviously in imaginative play, that is, play in which children generate roles, characters, objects, and plots. There is some evidence that viewing television is associated with low levels of these forms of imaginative play. J. L. Singer et al. (1984) found a negative relation between total viewing and imaginative play in the first year of a longitudinal study; during the subsequent years, the amount of viewing was unrelated to creativity. Program content appeared to be important, however, in that viewing violence was consistently associated with low creativity even when total television viewing was not.

The visualization hypothesis has been tested in experimental studies comparing responses to stories presented in televised form with the same text in an audio or print version (Greenfield & Beagles-Roos, 1988;

69

Greenfield, Farrar, & Beagles-Roos, 1986; Kerns, 1981; Meline, 1976; Runco & Pezdek, 1984; Valkenburg & Beentjes, 1997; Vibbert & Meringoff, 1981). With one exception, viewing a televised presentation resulted in fewer novel responses to the presentation than did listening to or reading a story. Because creative responses were generally defined as being different from information explicitly presented, these results may be accounted for by better memory for the details of the televised stories (Anderson & Collins, 1988). In one of the studies (Valkenburg & Beentjes, 1997), participants listened to the audio presentation twice. Although memory for the story improved, responses were still more creative (i.e., different from the content presented) than were those of participants who watched the story on television. This study was interpreted as supporting the hypothesis that the explicit visual images of television supplant internally generated imagery.

Of course, there are numerous reasons why television viewing and creativity might be negatively related without viewing's playing a causal role. Creative children and adolescents may choose to watch less television or may watch more educational programs than do their less imaginative peers. In two correlational studies, adolescents who were more creative and artistic participated in more activities and consequently watched less television (Richards, 1992; Wade, 1971). Moreover, divergent thinking predicted low viewing even after controlling for gender, SES, and intelligence (Furu, 1971).

MEASURES

Creative thinking was operationally defined as divergent thinking, or the ability to think about things in many different ways. Divergent thinking was measured with the verbal ideational fluency test (Alternate Uses of an Object) used by L. F. Harrison and Williams (1986). This form of creativity was explored because it has been found to yield the most convincing evidence of a relation between creativity and television viewing. The measure also allows us to compare our findings to those of L. F. Harrison and Williams (1986). Finally, the procedure lends itself to telephone administration. We also measured adolescents' participation in creative arts as additional indices of creativity.

The Alternate Uses of an Object Test

In the Alternate Uses of an Object Test, respondents were asked to think of different uses for each of three objects (a shoe, a key, and a tire). In the initial instructions, examples of various uses for a newspaper were provided (e.g., swat flies, start a fire). Participants were prompted to take more time if they reported that they could not think of any uses. Up to six responses were recorded. On average, participants generated three uses for each object (key, shoe, and tire). Correlations among items as well as a test of internal consistency indicated that these three items could be summed to a total creativity score (r = .47, .51, .50, all ps < .001 and Cronbach's alpha = .74).

In the standardization of this measure, both quantity (fluency) and quality (originality) of ideas were scored; the two were highly correlated (Milgram, Milgram, Rosenbloom, & Rabkin, 1978). Therefore, we coded only ideational fluency. Participants received one point for each answer that was distinct from others already given. If a subject gave a duplicate use (e.g., house decoration for a shoe and a key), only one point was awarded. The total score was the sum of responses across three objects. Three coders independently coded responses of six respondents. Agreement among pairs of coders was 97%, 97%, and 93%.

The test-retest reliability of the Alternate Uses test was evaluated in the interviews conducted with a subsample 1 year after their first interview (see Chapter 2). Items were changed from a shoe, key, and tire to a comb, spoon, and cardboard tube so that respondents would not base their responses on memory for the first test. Agreement among four coders averaged 89%. The correlation between scores from the original interview and those from the second interview was .58. Scores from the original interview were used in the analyses.

Creative Activities

Two additional measures were designed to assess involvement in creative activities in high school. In the interview, participants reported how often (number of days per week, then amount of time on those days) they participated in school-related and non-school-related activities and what these activities were. Participation in visual arts, music, drama, and journalism was coded as creative extracurricular activity; the participation score was the number of such activities named. The number of art classes taken (as a proportion of years in high school) was taken from high school transcripts.

RESULTS

Sex and Site Variations in Creativity

Boys had higher total verbal fluency scores (M = 9.29, SD = 3.76) than did girls (M = 8.64, SD = 3.98). The sex difference was probably due to boys' being able to name approximately one more alternate use for a tire than girls. Because the sum of total uses was positively skewed, a square-root transformation was used to stabilize the variance of this variable.

71

On average, teens reported participating in less than one (.65) creative or literary activity per year (range = 0 to 7). The maximum value was recoded to 3 because this variable was skewed and fewer than 3% of teens participated in more than three such activities. Participation varied by gender, $F(1,566) = 18.61$, $p < .001$; females participated in a greater number of creative activities ($M = .76$, $SD = .94$) than did males ($M = .45$, $SD = .77$).

The proportion of art classes taken in high school varied by sex, $F(1,487) = 19.04$, $p < .001$, and site, $F(1,487) = 41.58$, $p < .001$, with a significant sex by site interaction, $F(1,487) = 5.76$, $p < .05$. The means were KS males = .07, MA males = .04, KS females = .12, MA females = .06.

The zero-order correlations among the three creativity measures were modest. Participation in creative activities was positively associated with ideational fluency ($r = .18$, $p < .001$) and taking art classes ($r = .45$, $p < .001$). Ideational fluency was not significantly related to taking art classes ($r = .03$). Hence, the measures appear to assess somewhat different aspects of creativity. The measures of creativity were largely independent of academic achievement. In regressions of creativity measures on grades (controlling background variables of site, sex, parents' education, and number of older siblings), only the beta for creative extracurricular activities was significant ($\beta = .15$, $p < .001$).

The relations of creativity to leisure time book use were examined because some theorists argue that reading, like creativity, requires active cognitive processing that is different from that required for television viewing (e.g., T. M. Williams, 1986). There were small significant relations of book reading with each of the three measures of creativity with background characteristics controlled ($\beta s = .13$, .14, 17, all $p s < .01$).

Viewing as a Predictor of Creativity

The hierarchical regression models predicting the creativity measures were identical to those described in Chapter 4. In the analyses predicting participation in creative activities, time spent on chores and work was entered in addition to the other controls because it could limit the amount of time available for creative activities and for teen viewing.

Total Amount of Viewing

The results of regressions testing preschool and teen viewing are shown in Table 22. Preschool viewing time predicted low ideational fluency for girls, and teen viewing time predicted low ideational fluency for boys. Viewing time was unrelated to participation in creative extracurricular activities, but heavy preschool viewers took fewer art classes than light viewers did.

TABLE 22

SUMMARY OF REGRESSION ANALYSES PREDICTING CREATIVITY FROM TOTAL
PRESCHOOL AND TEEN TELEVISION VIEWING

	Ideational fluency			Creative activities	Proportion of art classes
	Both sexes	Male	Female	Both sexes	Both sexes
Background					
Parent education	.19***	.14*	.24***	.20***	.05
Birth order	−.05	−.03	−.07	−.05	−.03
Sex (female)	−.04	—	—	−.17***	−.17***
Site (MA)	−.02	−.05	.003	.06	.27***
Site × Sex	−.03	—	—	−.02	−.11**
Television					
Preschool total	−.03	.10	−.14**	−.06	−.11**
Teen total	−.07	−.19***	.03	.01	.003
Interactions					
Sex × Preschool Total	.52***	—	—	—	—
Sex × Teen Total	−.13**	—	—	—	—
Adjusted R^2	.09***	.06***	.10***	.07***	.13***

Note. Entries are standardized regression coefficients and adjusted R^2 values.
‡$p < .10$. *$p < .05$. **$p < .01$. ***$p < .001$.

Viewing Diet and Ideational Fluency

Regressions testing the relations of preschool informative, violent, and other entertainment viewing to each creativity measure were calculated, then the full model including both preschool and teen viewing diets was tested. With only the preschool viewing diet in the model, child informative viewing was positively related to ideational fluency, adjusted $R^2 = .09$, $p < .001$, $\beta = .08$, $p < .05$, and "other" program viewing was negatively related to ideational fluency, $\beta = −.09$, $p < .05$, but the latter effect was qualified by a significant interaction of Sex × Other Television, $\beta = .31$, $p < .05$.

These findings were essentially replicated in the analysis that included teen viewing, shown in Table 23, except that the main effect of child informative viewing was no longer significant. For boys, child informative viewing predicted ideational fluency at a borderline level of significance, providing slight support for the early learning model. For girls, viewing other entertainment in the preschool years was associated with lower ideational fluency, supporting the passivity hypothesis. In the adolescent years, boys who watched a lot of entertainment television had relatively low fluency scores, but girls who watched a lot of violent programs had relatively high scores (see Table 23).

TABLE 23

	Both sexes ($N = 570$)	Male ($N = 287$)	Female ($N = 283$)
Background			
Parent education	.18***	.12	.23***
Birth order	−.03	−.02	−.04
Site	.14	−.04	−.003
Sex	.18	—	—
Site × Sex	−.01	—	—
Preschool TV			
Informative	.07	.11‡	.03
Violent	.02	.03	.01
Other	−.08	.01	−.18*
Teen TV			
Informative	.04	−.004	.08
Violent	.06	−.08	.13*
Other	−.10*	−.20**	−.03
Interactions			
Sex × Preschool Other	.34*	—	—
Sex × Teen Violent	−.29**	—	—
Adjusted R^2	.14***	.05**	.10***

‡$p < .10.$ *$p < .05.$ **$p < .01.$ ***$p < .001.$

Viewing Diet and Creative Activities

Teens who had watched a lot of child informative programs in pre-school participated in more creative activities and took more art classes in high school than did infrequent viewers. The regressions are shown in Table 24. These overall effects were qualified by significant interactions with site. The association of child informative viewing with creative activities and art classes was significant for the Kansas teens but not for the Massachusetts teens. The site difference may result from the fact that Massachusetts teens took a smaller proportion of art classes and had smaller variance on that variable than did Kansas teens. For Kansas youth, teen viewing of informative programs also predicted greater participation in creative activities.

By contrast, teens who had viewed a lot of violence in preschool were less likely than low viewers to participate in creative activities or to take art classes. This pattern was also more pronounced for Kansas teens than for Massachusetts youth (see Table 24). For Massachusetts girls, however, high viewers of violence in the teen years took more art classes than low viewers. For these same females, those who viewed relatively little "other" entertainment programs in preschool tended to take more art classes.

TABLE 24

SUMMARY OF REGRESSION ANALYSES PREDICTING CREATIVE ACTIVITIES AND ART CLASSES
FROM PRESCHOOL AND TEEN INFORMATIVE, VIOLENT, AND OTHER TELEVISION

	Creative activities			Proportion art classes		
	Both sites	KS	MA	Both sites	KS	MA
Background						
Parent education	.19***	.08	.27***	.01	−.02	.03
Birth order	−.01	−.03	−.01	.01	.04	−.02
Site (MA)	.03	—	—	.15	—	—
Sex (female)	−.14***	−.12*	−.18**	−.15	−.21**	−.09
Site × Sex	.03	—	—	−.08	—	—
Work time	.06	.10‡	.01	—	—	—
Chore time	−.02	−.02	−.03	—	—	—
Preschool TV						
Informative	.14**	.22***	.03	.15**	.22**	.03
Violent	−.13*	−.23**	.00	−.13*	−.12	−.11
Other	−.03	−.06	−.03	−.09	−.07	−.14‡
Teen TV						
Informative	.13**	.22***	.04	.05	.06	.07
Violent	.03	.00	.07	.03	.08	.19**
Other	−.03	−.07	.00	−.04	−.05	−.03
Interactions						
Site × Preschool Informative	.34*	—	—	.36*	—	—
Site × Preschool Violent	−.35*	—	—	−.01	—	—
Site × Teen Informative	.22*	—	—	.05	—	—
Site × Teen Violent	−.07	—	—	−.26*	—	—
Adjusted R^2	.17***	.23***	.11***	.21***	.11***	.06**

‡$p < .10$. *$p < .05$. **$p < .01$. ***$p < .001$.

Content of Child Informative Programming

The two preschool programs that were most watched by our participants were *Sesame Street* and *Mister Rogers' Neighborhood*. These programs have been hypothesized to have different influences on children's creativity because of differences in program content, form, and design (e.g., Tower et al., 1979).

Mister Rogers' Neighborhood has a host who talks directly to the audience, presents only a few themes, has a slow pace, and incorporates long zoom techniques to focus on objects. The program also makes clear the distinction between fantasy and reality and encourages pretending and imagination (J. L. Singer & Singer, 1981). During our subjects' preschool years, one of the other child informative programs was *Captain Kangaroo*, which was also fairly slow in pace (Huston et al., 1981) and in which pretend and imagination were also central themes.

Sesame Street is produced in a magazine format with about 40 segments per 1-hr episode that vary in form and content. According to the pacing hypothesis, the magazine format reduces the reflection and active cognition that is necessary for creative development (J. L. Singer & Singer, 1979). Moreover, the curriculum does not emphasize pretending and imagination.

Hence, both the early learning hypothesis and the pacing hypotheses lead to the prediction that viewing *Mister Rogers*, and perhaps other child informative programs, will be more likely to predict creativity than will *Sesame Street* viewing. We tested *Mister Rogers, Sesame Street*, and other child informative programs as predictors of adolescent creativity. Adolescent viewing was not included because there are no parallel programs in general-audience programming. Regression analyses, shown in Table 25, indicated that *Mister Rogers* viewing was consistently and positively related to ideational fluency for the entire sample. Viewing both *Mister Rogers* and other child informative programs predicted participation in creative activities, but slightly more strongly for the Kansas site than for the Massachusetts teens. These programs were not consistently related to taking art classes (analysis not shown).

Sesame Street viewing was unrelated to ideational fluency or to participating in creative activities. It did predict taking art classes, but this effect

TABLE 25

SUMMARY OF REGRESSION ANALYSES PREDICTING IDEATIONAL FLUENCY AND CREATIVE
ACTIVITIES FROM SPECIFIC TYPES OF CHILD INFORMATIVE TELEVISION

	Ideational fluency	Creative activities		
	Both sites	Both sites	KS	MA
Background				
Parent education	.20***	.21***	.14*	.27***
Birth order	−.03	−.03	−.04	−.02
Sex (female)	.09**	−.18***	−.21***	−.17**
Site (MA)	.00	−.50**	—	—
Site × Sex	.00	−.03	—	—
Work time	—	.06	.12‡	.01
Chore time	—	.00	.01	−.01
Preschool informative TV				
Mister Rogers	.10**	.12**	.15*	.08
Sesame Street	−.04	.00	.08	−.09
Other	.03	.09*	.08	.04
Interactions				
Site × *Sesame Street*	—	.28*	—	—
Adjusted R^2	.07***	.11***	.10***	.09***

‡$p < .10$. *$p < .05$. **$p < .01$. ***$p < .001$.

was complicated by interactions with site and gender. The patterns varied considerably across site and sex in ways that are not readily interpretable (βs ranged from $-.20$, *ns*, for MA males to .31, $p < .001$, for KS females; R^2s for KS males and MA females were not significant).

CONCLUSIONS

These results suggest that content is the most important predictor of television's relations to ideational fluency, participation in creative activities, and taking art classes. Viewing diet accounted for more variance than did total television viewing for all three dependent measures, even with adjustment for the number of predictors in the model. Most indicators of creativity were higher for teens who had watched a lot of educational television as preschoolers than for infrequent viewers.

The early learning hypothesis received further support from the analysis comparing different child informative programs. Viewing *Mister Rogers' Neighborhood,* which is especially oriented to stimulating imagination and pretense, specifically predicted ideational fluency, and both *Mister Rogers* and other child informative programs positively predicted participation in creative activities. Many of these other children's informative programs also emphasize creativity (Neapolitan & Huston, 1994). By contrast, *Sesame Street* emphasizes preacademic cognitive, language, and social skills. Viewing *Sesame Street* predicts academic achievement more consistently than viewing other child informative programs does (Chapter 4), but *Sesame Street* viewing is much less consistently related to creativity. These findings support the proposition that programs with different curricula and goals can contribute to different positive outcomes.

Hypotheses predicting overall negative relations of television viewing to creativity were not well supported. The strongest evidence against these interpretations is that time spent with child informative programming is positively associated with teen creativity. If some programming fosters creativity, whereas other programming is inimical to it, then neither simple time spent with television nor the visual qualities of the medium are useful explanations of television's relation to creativity.

The violent content hypothesis receives some support from the findings that preschool viewing of violent programming has negative associations with later creativity. Assuming that superficial entertainment programs induce passivity, but cognitively challenging educational programs do not, a modified version of the passivity hypothesis also receives some support, at least in the domain of ideational fluency.

The proposal that slow pacing encourages imagination and rapid pacing discourages it is partially supported by the finding that viewing *Mister*

Rogers' Neighborhood predicted ideational fluency and participation in creative activities. The other side of the pacing hypothesis, that the rapid pace of *Sesame Street* interferes with creativity, was not supported. For the most part, *Sesame Street* viewing was unrelated to creativity; there was no evidence of a negative relation. It is possible, however, that the negative relations of viewing violent programs to measures of creativity were a function of rapid pace rather than violence. Most of the violent programs viewed in preschool were cartoons, which have a more rapid pace and higher rates of visual and auditory special effects than does *Sesame Street* (Huston et al., 1981; Huston & Wright, 1994).

We suggested earlier that the hypothesis that television viewing induces both physical and intellectual passivity would be more likely to apply to general entertainment programs than to child informative programs. General entertainment (e.g., comedies, adult game shows) may be relatively uninvolving for a young child and therefore undemanding and unlikely to stimulate imagination or divergent thought. Viewing general entertainment in preschool predicted low ideational fluency among females, and teen viewing of such programs was related to low fluency for males. Our results thus provide very modest support for a modified version of the passivity hypothesis.

SUMMARY

The total amount of preschool viewing was associated with lower ideational fluency for girls and to taking relatively few art classes for the whole sample. For males, total teen viewing was associated with lower ideational fluency. These patterns appeared to be accounted for primarily by general entertainment programming. Adolescents who had watched a lot of child informative programs as preschoolers scored slightly better on ideational fluency, participated in more creative activities, and took more art classes. Viewing *Mister Rogers' Neighborhood* was more consistently related to creativity than was viewing *Sesame Street*. Preschool violence viewing was negatively related to creative participation, but viewing violence in high school was positively associated with some indicators of creativity for females.

VI. AGGRESSION

Television violence and aggression are more studied than any other topic in the television literature. The consensus among most social scientists who have reviewed this literature is that there is a causal relation between viewing violence and aggressive behavior (e.g., Comstock & Paik, 1991; Condry, 1989; Dubow & Miller, 1996; Huston & Wright, 1997; Liebert & Sprafkin, 1988; Pearl, Bouthilet, & Lazar, 1982). Several theoretical issues, however, remain less clearly resolved. How durable or lasting are the effects of viewing? Does viewing in early childhood have particularly important effects on later behavior or attitudes? What are the processes that mediate or moderate long-term viewing effects?

HYPOTHESES BASED ON CONTENT

Violent Content

Both observational learning and information processing theories, described in Chapter 1, predict that exposure to television violence, especially during the early years, has long-term effects on patterns of aggressive attitudes and responses to environmental provocation (Bandura, 1977, 1994; Huesmann, 1986; Huesmann & Miller, 1994). One important prediction from information processing theory is that exposure to television violence in early childhood may be especially important because young children have few preexisting scripts for many types of social conflict or problem situations. They are therefore less likely than older children to have alternative scripts. Continued viewing leads children to retrieve, rehearse, solidify, and expand existing scripts, resulting in cumulative long-term effects.

Prosocial Content

Prosocial television often contains messages about nonviolent conflict resolution, empathy, helping, sharing, and negotiating. Social learning and information processing theories predict that such prosocial content can lower aggression by providing children with alternative means of dealing with interpersonal conflict. In early experimental studies, there was support for positive effects of prosocial television on prosocial behavior, but children in the experimental groups did not show significantly less aggression than those in control conditions (Collins & Getz, 1976; Friedrich & Stein, 1973). In the one meta-analysis that included prosocial television, there was a tendency for viewing prosocial television to predict low levels of antisocial behavior (effect size comparing prosocial television to "other" was −.20), but the outcomes included stereotyping and materialism as well as aggression. When the whole viewing diet was considered, the effect size comparing antisocial and prosocial television was .65 (Hearold, 1986). When our participants were 5 years old, the age-appropriate programs with the most clearly prosocial content were also the programs we have designated child informative, especially *Sesame Street* and *Mister Rogers' Neighborhood.*

HYPOTHESES BASED ON TELEVISION AS A MEDIUM

Most of the theories about the influences of television as a medium have not been directed at its effects on aggressive behavior or attitudes. Theories focusing on the formal features of television, however, do lead to the prediction that exposure to programming with rapid pace, high levels of activity, and frequent use of visual and auditory special effects can produce arousal, which may activate aggressive behavior. Cartoons, the most violent programs for children, also have very high rates of potentially arousing formal features, so viewing them could increase aggression through general arousal as well as through specific violent content messages (J. L. Singer & Singer, 1981; Wright & Huston, 1983). Although *Sesame Street* has lower rates of arousing formal features than do typical cartoons (Huston & Wright, 1994), some theories suggest that its rapid pacing could stimulate aggression, whereas the slow pacing of *Mister Rogers' Neighborhood* would not do so. As arousal effects dissipate fairly rapidly, one would expect long-term effects only if arousal led to repeated aggressive behavior that eventually became habitual.

REVIEW OF EARLIER RESEARCH

Four meta-analyses best summarize prior research (Andison, 1977; Hearold, 1986; Paik & Comstock, 1994; Wood, Wong, & Chachere, 1991). All concluded that viewing violence is related to aggression, but their estimates of effect size varied considerably. The analyses by Hearold (1986) include not only aggression as an outcome but materialism and stereotyping as well. Paik and Comstock (1994) limited the outcome measures to behaviors that were clearly aggressive (i.e., self-reports of aggressive intention, observed aggressive behavior in laboratory simulations or real-world situations, and illegal behavior). The overall effect size was .65 when multiple contrasts within studies were included; with each study entered only once, it was .73. Such effect sizes are quite large in social science research.

Experiments and Quasi-Experiments

Wood et al. (1991) restricted their meta-analysis to experiments with random assignment in which the dependent measure was aggression toward another person who was physically present. For the total sample of 28 experiments, there was a significant effect of viewing violence on aggression. Effect sizes could be calculated for 12 studies; they were 0.27 weighted for sample size and 0.40 unweighted.

In one quasi-experiment comparing towns with and without access to television, children's levels of aggression were initially similar across towns; in the town without television, however, the average levels of physical aggression increased after television became available. Moreover, individual differences in amount of television viewing predicted changes in physical aggression over time (Joy, Kimball, & Zabrock, 1986). Because arousing form and violent content are highly correlated in television, it is not possible to determine their relative contributions to aggressive outcomes. In one series of experiments, children's aggressive behavior increased after exposure to programs with high rates of nonviolent action *and* after those with violent content (Huston & Wright, 1989). Overall, experimental and quasi-experimental studies provide strong support for the effects of violent television on physical aggression, but other features of typical television programs may contribute to these effects.

Longitudinal Studies

Longitudinal analyses are most pertinent to the issue of whether effects of viewing are durable and generalized. Three different studies included similar measures of viewing and aggression. Milavsky, Stipp, Kessler, and Rubens (1982) measured these variables for elementary school boys and girls and for teenage boys on multiple occasions over 3 years. Regressions were used to determine whether viewing at one occasion predicted aggression at the next occasion with prior aggression statistically controlled. Most of the coefficients were positive but did not reach statistical significance. The authors concluded that there were no effects of viewing.

81

Others, however, concluded that the pattern of coefficients did indicate positive effects (Cook, Kendziersky, & Thomas, 1983).

Among boys assessed at ages 8 and 18 in another investigation, preference for television violence at age 8 predicted aggression at age 18 (Eron, Lefkowitz, Huesmann, & Walder, 1972). When the sample was studied again at age 30, viewing violence at age 8 predicted convictions for violent crime at age 30 (this finding is somewhat tenuous because of reduced sample size; Huesmann & Miller, 1994). There were no significant relations for females.

In the 1980s, a group of parallel studies was conducted in the United States, Poland, Israel (both kibbutz and city), Australia, and Finland (Huesmann & Eron, 1986; Huesmann & Miller, 1994). First- and third-grade children were followed for 2 years. Violence viewing was measured by children's reports, and aggression was assessed by peer nominations. There were positive relations between viewing and aggressive behavior for boys in all countries except those in an Israeli kibbutz. Viewing violence in earlier grades predicted later aggression; coefficients were statistically significant in four of six comparisons. Similar patterns occurred for girls in all except one sample (Australia), but the coefficients were statistically significant in only two of the six comparisons, one of which was the United States. There were no instances in which violence viewing was significantly negatively related to aggression. These studies also provided evidence for a bidirectional effect of violence viewing and behavior; that is, in most samples, early measures of aggression also predicted later viewing of violence.

These analyses included controls for social status, children's achievement level, and parental behavior as well as several measures of children's attitudes and beliefs. In a similar study in the Netherlands, Wiegerman, Kuttschreuter, and Baarda (1992) concluded that the correlation between viewing and aggression was largely a result of the effects of intelligence on both processes. As their measure of intelligence was not collected before the viewing measure, the causal direction is difficult to determine, but their hypothesis deserves further investigation.

Moderators of Viewing Effects

Gender

Boys watch more violent television than do girls (Huston & Wright, 1997), and boys, on average, are more aggressive than are girls (Maccoby & Jacklin, 1974). Some theories predict greater effects of television violence for boys because of their apparently greater susceptibility to aggressive problem solutions and because male television characters perform more violent actions than do female television characters. Most experimental studies, however, show that females and males are both affected by viewing violent or aggressive television. In longitudinal studies, the results are mixed. For children studied initially in the 1950s, viewing at age 8 predicted aggression at age 18 only for males (Eron et al., 1972). For children studied in the 1970s, however, violent television viewing predicted aggression for girls as well as for boys (Huesmann & Eron, 1986).

An alternative line of reasoning predicts stronger effects of viewing violence for girls than for boys and stronger effects of prosocial television for boys than for girls. Gender role expectations in virtually all societies include aggression as a sex-appropriate behavior for males but not for females. Hence, young boys may be exposed to more socialization experiences that encourage the development of aggression than are young girls. Individual differences in exposure to television violence, therefore, might play a larger role in the socialization of aggression for females, whereas exposure to prosocial content might have more impact on individual differences for boys. That is, when television provides content that runs counter to sex-stereotyped expectations, it may have more impact than when it simply adds to the many cultural and socialization influences that channel children into sex-typed patterns of behavior. (This same hypothesis was used in Chapter 4 to explain sex differences in relations of preschool viewing to teen academic achievement.)

Identification With Television Characters

Extensive viewing can lead children to identify with television characters. Such identification may make the viewer especially receptive to encoding and adopting the behaviors displayed by those characters. There is evidence from several studies that viewing is correlated with identification, especially for boys (Fernie, 1981; Huesmann & Eron, 1986). Moreover, the relation of viewing to aggression 1 and 2 years later was strongest for boys who identified with television characters in the studies by Huesmann and Eron (1986) in the United States and Lagerspetz and Viemero (1986) in Finland.

Intellectual Achievement

Intelligence and early school achievement have been proposed as both mediators and moderators of viewing effects. Low intelligence could lead to both high viewing and high aggression, producing a spurious association between them (Wiegerman et al., 1992). Intelligence could also moderate the effects of viewing: More intelligent children might be less vulnerable than less intelligent children to the negative influences of viewing violence because they are less likely to consider it realistic or useful in real life.

MEASURES

Violent and Prosocial Television

We defined preschool exposure to television violence as the time spent at age 5 viewing children's cartoons and general-audience action-adventure programs and exposure to prosocial content as the time spent viewing child informative programs (see Chapter 2).

Aggression

The aggression scale was composed of eight items adapted from Buss and Durkee (1957). These items were drawn from the following original subscales: assault (e.g., "When someone insults you or your family, do you feel they are asking for a fight?"), verbal aggression (e.g., "When people yell at you, do you yell back?"), indirect aggression (e.g., "When you are angry, do you slam doors?"), and irritability (e.g., "Do you let a lot of unimportant things irritate you?"). Each item was answered on a 5-point Likert-type scale: *never, rarely, sometimes, often,* or *very often.* The Cronbach alpha for the study sample was .74.

Television Focus

One additional measure was collected only for the Kansas sample at age 5. The child's television focus consisted of parent ratings on 15 items using 5-point Likert-type scales describing how often the child asked questions or talked about television, played television characters and themes, or otherwise brought television content into daily life. The Cronbach alpha for the scale was .82.

RESULTS

Viewing as a Predictor of Aggression

Because there were different patterns of effects by gender, we report all analyses separately for males and females. All include controls for parent education, birth order, and site. The regression models included the preschool viewing diet (child informative, violent, and other programs) and the teen viewing diet (adult informative, violent, and other programs). The results are summarized in Table 26.

Males who were heavy viewers of child informative programs were less aggressive in adolescence than those who rarely watched educational programs during their preschool years. Exposure to television violence in the

TABLE 26

SUMMARY OF REGRESSIONS PREDICTING TEEN AGGRESSION FROM VIEWING
IN PRESCHOOL AND TEEN YEARS FOR MALE AND FEMALE

| | Male | Female | | |
	Both sites	KS	MA	Both sites
Background				
Parent education	−.08	−.01	−.09	−.06
Birth order	−.01	.14	−.03	.04
Site (MA)	.00	—	—	−.23*
Preschool TV				
Informative	−.20***	−.03	.10	−.10
Violent	.07	.21‡	−.10	.50*
Other	.07	−.01	−.06	−.18
Teen TV				
Informative	−.03	−.03	−.15‡	.14
Violent	.00	−.05	.17*	−.24
Other	.00	−.06	.21*	−.32
Interactions				
Site × Preschool Violent	—	—	—	−.61*
Site × Teen Other	—	—	—	.64*
Adjusted R^2	.032*	.060	.144**	.047*

Note. Entries are standardized beta weights. Two outliers were excluded.
‡$p < .10$. *$p < .05$. **$p < .01$. ***$p < .001$.

preschool years was not a significant predictor of aggression, nor was viewing violence in the teen years.

For females, the relations between viewing and aggression varied by
site. Separate analyses for the two sites are shown in Table 26. For Kansas
females, viewing was unrelated to aggression. For females in the Massachusetts site, those who viewed violent and other entertainment television
as teens had relatively high levels of aggression; those who viewed informative television in the teen years had relatively low levels of aggression.

Individual Differences in Involvement With Television

In earlier studies, the long-term relations of viewing violence to later
childhood and adult behavior were most pronounced for males who had
identified with television characters in childhood (Huesmann & Eron,
1986; Huesmann & Miller, 1994). The closest parallel measure in our
preschool data was television focus. We expected that children who scored
high on television focus would be those who were most likely to identify
with television characters and therefore to be influenced by the content
they viewed.

To test this hypothesis, Kansas children were divided into three groups based on the preschool television focus score: high (n = 94, 61 boys), medium (n = 71, 38 boys), and low (n = 71, 29 boys). The interaction of preschool exposure to violence with television focus was included as a predictor of teen aggression. The interaction was significant, β = 1.67, p < .05. To clarify the nature of this interaction, separate regressions of teen aggression on preschool exposure to violence were performed for each level of television focus. Males and females were combined because none of the main effects or interactions involving gender was significant and the cell sizes for the two sexes separately would have been quite small. It should be noted, however, that the proportion of males is higher in the high television focus group than in the low television focus group.

In Model 1 (Table 27), only the three preschool viewing categories were included because adding the teen viewing categories would have made the number of predictors very large for the small sample sizes. For children with high and medium levels of television focus, viewing violence in preschool was a significant predictor of teen aggression. That is, for children in the top two thirds of the distribution on a measure of talking about television and using television themes in play, those who watched more violence in preschool were more aggressive as teenagers. For children with low levels of television focus, there was not a significant relation between viewing violence in preschool and teen aggression.

TABLE 27

SUMMARY OF REGRESSIONS PREDICTING TEEN AGGRESSION FROM VIEWING IN PRESCHOOL AND TEEN YEARS FOR CHILDREN WITH DIFFERENT LEVELS OF TELEVISION FOCUS IN EARLY CHILDHOOD, KANSAS SITE ONLY

	Model 1			Model 2		
	TV focus					
	Low	Medium	High	Low	Medium	High
Background						
Parent education	.06	−.01	−.28*	.05	.05	−.27*
Birth order	.26	.18	−.07	.26*	.24*	−.05
Sex (female)	−.37	−.23	.06	−.30*	−.26*	.05
Preschool TV						
Informative	.03	−.16	−.13	—	—	—
Violent	−.12	.24*	.24*	−.05	.14	.24*
Other	.03	−.14	.01	—	—	—
Teen TV						
Violent	—	—	—	−.10	.21‡	.04
Adjusted R^2	.064	.111*	.088*	.051	.145**	.091*

Note. Low N = 72; Medium N = 71; High N = 95. Entries are standardized regression coefficients and adjusted R^2 values.

‡p < .10. *p < .05. **p < .01.

In Model 2 (Table 27) we tested only violence viewing at each age level without the other viewing categories in order to determine whether teen viewing was a mediator of the relations of preschool viewing to teen aggression. The mediational role of teen viewing was supported for the medium television focus group but not for the high television focus group. For children high on television focus as preschoolers, preschool violence viewing was significantly related to aggression; teen viewing made almost no contribution. For children with medium levels of television focus, teen viewing was a significant predictor, and preschool viewing was positively but no longer significantly related to aggression.

Parallel analyses of child informative viewing showed no interactions of viewing with television focus. Because of the small number of subjects in each group, no analyses including all six preschool and teen viewing categories were performed.

Intelligence

Does Intelligence Mediate the Relation of Viewing to Aggression?

We tested the hypothesis that intelligence determines both viewing and aggression, accounting for their relation to one another, using scores on the PPVT-R administered at age 5 (see Chapter 2 for description). The partial correlations of PPVT-R with viewing and violence, controlling for parent education, were nonsignificant for the sample as a whole and for males and females separately, so there was no evidence that verbal intelligence mediated the association. Preschool viewing of child informative programs was related to PPVT-R scores ($r = .17$, $p < .001$), especially for males (male $r = .25$, $p < .001$; female $r = .10$, ns). Regressions including PPVT-R (not shown) indicated that it did not account for the relations of child informative viewing to teen aggression.

Does Intelligence Moderate Relations of Viewing to Aggression?

The hypothesis that more intellectually competent children might respond to television messages differently than less competent children was evaluated by testing the interactions of PPVT-R with violence viewing and with child informative viewing. None of the interactions was significant.

Sesame Street, Mister Rogers' Neighborhood, and Other Child Informative Programs

We examined the relations of specific child informative programs to teen aggression to test the hypothesis that their form and content would have different effects on young children. The results appear in Table 28. For males, *Sesame Street* viewing predicted lower aggression and *Mister Rogers* viewing was unrelated to aggression. The relation of other child informative programs was modified by an interaction with site; as we had no specific hypothesis about this category of program, no subsequent analyses were performed. For girls, the viewing variables did not account for a significant proportion of the variance.

CONCLUSIONS

The findings provided only partial support for the observational and information processing theories. There were no overall relations between violence viewing at age 5 and the participants' aggressive attitudes, and there were few relations of teen violence viewing to aggression. Our failure to replicate earlier longitudinal findings (e.g., Eron et al., 1972) is surprising and may be due to an insufficient measure of teen aggression. Although our measures of preschool viewing were more extensive and refined than those in most earlier research, our measure of aggression was brief and was based entirely on self-report. Moreover, it included indirect aggression, verbal aggression, irritability, and physical aggression. The most clear-cut findings in earlier studies have occurred for physical aggression. Nevertheless, we found some interesting relations of viewing to our measure of aggression.

TABLE 28

SUMMARY OF REGRESSIONS PREDICTING TEEN AGGRESSION FROM VIEWING DIFFERENT CATEGORIES OF CHILD INFORMATIVE PROGRAMS IN PRESCHOOL

	Male	Female[a]
Background		
Parent education	−.11‡	−.05
Birth order	.000	.02
Site (MA)	−.65*	−.42
Preschool informative TV		
Mister Rogers	.04	.00
Sesame Street	−.20**	.03
All other	.15*	.16‡
Interactions		
Site × All Other	.66***	.01
Adjusted R^2	.090***	.006

[a]excluding 1 outlier.
‡$p < .10$. *$p < .05$. **$p < .01$. ***$p < .001$.

The earlier finding that identification with television characters moderated the relations of viewing to aggression over a 2-year period (Huesmann & Eron, 1986) was replicated over a 10- to 12-year period in our results. For children who were rated medium and high on television focus as preschoolers, viewing violent programming in preschool was positively associated with aggression in adolescence. For children rated low on television focus, on the other hand, preschool violence viewing was unrelated to teen aggression. Although the high television focus children were more apt to be boys and the low television focus group were more apt to be girls, the absence of an interaction with child sex suggests that it is children's interest and involvement with television rather than gender per se that accounts for their different responses to violent programs. Children's overall involvement in television, which is manifested as they talk about television and use its themes in their play, may lead them to be especially susceptible to its violent content. The fascination with superheroes and elaborate play built on cartoon and adventure themes may magnify and provide opportunities for rehearsal both of the violent content shown in the programs and of the thoughts associated therewith.

For boys, content-related hypotheses were supported with respect to viewing child informative television; frequent viewers at age 5 had relatively low levels of teen aggression. Moreover, when child informative programs were examined separately, viewers of *Sesame Street* showed low levels of aggression. This finding is sensible insofar as *Sesame Street* has long included prosocial conflict resolution messages. This finding also contradicts assertions that aggressive messages or formal features of *Sesame Street* stimulate aggressive tendencies.

SUMMARY

Boys who were heavy viewers of child informative programs were less aggressive in adolescence than their peers who were light viewers. There was no overall relation between viewing violence in preschool and teen aggression; instead, that relation depended upon children's overall involvement with television in the preschool years. For those whose preschool play and conversation was heavily saturated with television characters and content, viewing violence at age 5 predicted teen aggression. For children with low involvement in television, the relation between preschool viewing and teen aggression was not significant.

VII. EXTRACURRICULAR ACTIVITIES

This chapter considers the relations of preschool and teen viewing to teens' participation in extracurricular activities. Extracurricular activities can provide opportunities for young people to develop social, intellectual, and athletic skills. Teens who participate in such activities are, for the most part, more likely to be involved in school and to perform better academically than those who do not (Eccles & Barber, 1999; Mahoney & Cairns, 1997; Pettit, Laird, Bates, & Dodge, 1997; Posner & Vandell, 1999).

HYPOTHESES BASED ON CONTENT

Stimulating Interests

Early television viewing could influence later participation in extracurricular activities because skills and habits acquired in early life can affect later behavioral choices. Preschool viewing of programs with educational and prosocial content might stimulate interests in academic, service, and creative pursuits. Watching *Reading Rainbow,* for example, stimulates children's interest in reading the books featured on the program, as evidenced by demand for these books in libraries (RMC Research Corporation, 1989).

In the teen years, adolescents' interests may lead them to pursue particular activities *and* particular media content. We have already seen in Chapter 3 that adolescents' patterns of television and print use appear to be guided by content rather than by medium. These findings are consistent with theories proposing that children and adolescents use media to satisfy particular motives, interests, and abilities at particular times (Rosengren et al., 1985). By extension, this view leads to the prediction that the content of media will be associated with the content of activities that a child or adolescent pursues. Using this perspective, one might expect an interest in current events to be associated with watching television news and documentaries and with participating in academic and leadership extracurricular activities. The avid athlete might participate in sports and watch sports television. Even if teens actively select media content on the basis of their interests, exposure may facilitate or inhibit involvement in activities. For example, viewing television programs about sports could both activate and result from active participation in sports. That is, the causal relations are most likely to be bidirectional: Television and print materials influence interests, and individuals select a variety of media that reflect or build upon their interests (Himmelweit, Oppenheim, & Vince, 1958; Neuman, 1991).

HYPOTHESES BASED ON TELEVISION AS A MEDIUM

Several of the theories described in Chapter 1 lead to the prediction that television as a medium will reduce children's and adolescents' involvement in academic, social, and athletic activities.

Cultivating Passivity

According to this view, because extensive early television viewing allegedly cultivates general intellectual and physical passivity, a child who spends a great deal of time with television in the early years will engage in less outdoor play, social interaction, and other activities away from home. These habits of time allocation will persist, affecting the choice of leisure activities in later childhood and adolescence. This reasoning leads to the prediction that preschool television viewing, regardless of content, will be associated with low participation in adolescent activities.

Displacement and Default

The most straightforward prediction from displacement theory is that the time spent viewing television displaces time in social and physical activity (e.g., participation in sports or social groups). Therefore, time spent viewing television will be negatively correlated with time spent in other important activities when the two are measured contemporaneously. Available studies do not support this prediction strongly. In two investigations of time use diaries kept by children and adolescents, time spent viewing television was unrelated to total time in most other activities (Carpenter, Huston, & Spera, 1989; Timmer et al., 1985). A stronger test of displacement comes from studies of the introduction of television in British Columbia (T. M. Williams, 1986), Australia (Murray & Kippax, 1978), and South Africa (Mutz et al., 1993). All three found some support for the hypothesis that television displaced outdoor activities, sports, and social activities away from home (Murray & Kippax, 1978; Mutz et al., 1993; T. M. Williams & Handford, 1986). In a longitudinal analysis conducted after television was well-established, however, there was a tendency for television viewing to be positively related to social interaction with both parents and peers at a later age (Rosengren & Windahl, 1989).

Even if television viewing were negatively related to participation in activities, the causal direction could be from activities to viewing. Adolescents who participate actively in extracurricular activities have less time to watch television; those who are not involved in outside activities have more time at home, where television viewing is a likely way of occupying time. The notion of television as default is supported by data showing that adults watch more television in the winter than the summer, but school-aged children increase viewing in the summer (Huston et al., 1999). For adolescents in Sweden, extensive leisure activities predicted lowered television viewing at a later age (Rosengren & Windahl, 1989).

Although processes of both displacement and default viewing probably occur under some circumstances, the relations of television viewing to other activities also depend in part on family patterns, cultural practices and expectations, and social structural conditions. For example, Japanese and Korean young people watch as much television as those in the United States do, but they read a little more, spend a lot more time on school-work, and participate in sports much less (Larson & Verma, 1998).

MEASURES

Participants were asked if they were involved in school-related and non-school-related activities. Time per week was obtained for both types of activities using the two-question format described earlier (number of days per week, then amount of time on those days). Participants also named the individual activities in which they took part. Regular classes (e.g., gym) were not included, but voluntary activities in school, such as student government, were counted. These were categorized as service and religious (e.g., environmental and nature clubs, church youth groups, community service), leadership and social (e.g., Junior Achievement, sorority, student government, military), creative and literary (plays and theater, music and arts, journalism), athletic (individual and team sports), academic and intellectual (e.g., debate, language clubs), and other. The score for each category was the number of activities named in that category. Work was defined as chores at home (e.g., housework or yard work) and work for pay. Time per week in each was calculated.

RESULTS

We first examined adolescents' participation in extracurricular activities as a function of total amount of television viewing to test the passivity, displacement, and default hypotheses. The next analyses were designed to test the hypothesis that adolescents who viewed television in particular content areas would participate in activities in those content domains.[3]

During the school year, participants reported spending an average of 10.86 hr per week in extracurricular activities (SD = 8.30), 1.95 hr in unpaid chores (primarily house and yard work; SD = 0.57), and almost 2.86 hr in paid work (SD = 1.43). On average, they participated in 3.34 different activities (SD = 2.36); the means were athletic = 1.24 (SD = 1.24), academic = .34 (SD = 0.77), creative = .65 (SD = 1.05), leadership = .25 (SD = 0.54), and service = .68 (SD = 0.87).

The zero-order correlations among paid and unpaid work and different types of extracurricular activities are shown in Table 29. In general, students who reported participation in any one type of activity among academic, creative, leadership, or service activities tended to be active in the other types of activities as well. Participation in athletic activities was not related to engaging in academic or creative activities but was related to being involved in leadership and service activities. Students who spent more time in paid work participated in fewer activities, particularly athletic and academic activities.

Total Viewing

The results of regressions testing the relations of preschool and adolescent total viewing time to activity participation and number of activities are shown in Table 30. Times spent in paid and unpaid work were included as controls in addition to parent education, birth order, sex, and site.

The amount of television viewed during the preschool years was unrelated to adolescent participation in extracurricular activities (both time and number). Adolescents who watched a lot of television participated in fewer activities than those who viewed less, but there was no difference in the time they reported devoting to extracurricular activities. There were no interactions with sex or site.

Program Content

To test the hypotheses that television content would be related to adolescents' interests and hence to their choice of extracurricular activities,

---

[3]Results for creative activities are reported in Chapter 5.

TABLE 29

Correlations Among Times in Work and Extracurricular Activities

	Paid work	Total hours	Total number	Extracurricular activities				
Category				Athletic (number)	Academic (number)	Creative (number)	Leadership (number)	Service (number)
Work								
Unpaid (hr/week)	.05	.002	-.03	-.09	-.01	-.02	-.01	.07
Paid (hr/week)	—	-.15***	-.11**	-.13*	-.12**	.01	.01	-.09*
Extracurricular activities								
Total hours		—	.54***	.50***	.12**	.25***	.11*	.21***
Total number			—	.56***	.48***	.49***	.39***	.60***
Athletic (number)				—	.02	-.03	.10*	.10*
Academic (number)					—	.17***	.19***	.19***
Creative (number)						—	.00	.19***
Leadership (number)							—	.22***
Service (number)								—

*p < .05. **p < .01. ***p < .001.

TABLE 30

SUMMARY OF REGRESSION ANALYSES PREDICTING EXTRACURRICULAR ACTIVITIES
FROM PRESCHOOL AND ADOLESCENT TOTAL TELEVISION VIEWING TIME

	Extracurricular activities	
	Total hours	Total number
Background		
Parent education	.14***	.26***
Birth order	.06	−.05
Sex (female)	.03	−.10*
Site (MA)	−.02	−.05
Sex × Site	.07‡	.10**
Time in paid work	−.15***	−.13**
Time in unpaid work	.05	0
Television		
Preschool total	−.03	0
Teen total	−.06	−.11**
Adjusted R^2	.041***	.135***

‡$p < .10$. *$p < .05$. **$p < .01$. ***$p < .001$.

television viewing diets were examined. The contents of television programs and activities were most clearly parallel for academic activities (informative television) and athletics (sports television). For academic activities, the preschool and teen viewing diets were divided into three categories: informative, violent, and all other. Although there were no specific predictions about differences between violent and other entertainment programs, these two viewing categories had different relations to other outcomes, suggesting that they might function differently in relation to students' interests and individual characteristics. Although the content parallels between informative television and service and leadership activities are a little less clear than for academic activities, participation in these activities may indicate interest in the wider world that would be associated with choosing informative television. The regression models tested the relations of preschool and adolescent television diets to participation in different types of activity. Hours spent in paid and unpaid work were again controlled. The results appear in Table 31.

Informative Content

Teens who often watched informative programs at either the preschool or adolescent assessments participated in more academic and service activities than did infrequent viewers. The relation of teen informative

TABLE 31

STANDARDIZED REGRESSION COEFFICIENTS FOR EXTRACURRICULAR ACTIVITIES
PREDICTED BY PRESCHOOL AND ADOLESCENT VIEWING DIET

	Number of activities		
	Academic	Leadership	Service
Background			
Parent education	.16***	.03	.11**
Birth order	−.07	−.03	−.02
Sex	.24	−.58*	−.13**
Site	−.25	−.36	−.02
Sex × Site	.33	.06	.15
Time in paid work	−.08*	.00	−.09*
Time in unpaid work	.00	−.03	.07
Preschool TV			
Informative	.09*	.01	.09*
Violent	.00	−.11*	−.05
Other	−.04	.12*	−.02
Teen TV			
Informative	.16***	.04	.09*
Violent	.08‡	−.12**	−.04
Other	−.05	−.10*	−.11**
Interactions			
Site × Preschool Other TV	.45**	.48**	—
Site × Teen Other TV	−.33*	.05	—
Sex × Preschool Violent	.59**	.27	—
Site × Sex × Preschool Informative TV	−.33*	—	—
Adjusted R^2	.10***	.05**	.097***

‡$p < .10$. *$p < .05$. **$p < .01$. ***$p < .001$.

viewing to these activities was consistent across subgroups, but there were interactions of preschool viewing with site and sex for academic activities. Separate analyses by site and sex produced inconsistent patterns. The positive relation of preschool child informative viewing to academic activities was significant only for Massachusetts males (β = .19, $p < .05$, adjusted R^2 = .12, $p < .01$).

Violent Content

Viewing violent content at either the preschool or adolescent time periods was negatively associated with participation in leadership activities. The interaction of Preschool Violence Viewing × Sex was significant in the analysis for academic activities. Viewing violence was slightly positively related to academic activities for males (βs: KS males = .17, $p < .10$;

MA males = .15, *ns*) and negatively related for Kansas females (βs: KS females = −.32, *p* < .01; MA females = −.04, *ns*)

Other Entertainment Programs

Preschool viewing of "other" entertainment programs was associated with greater participation in leadership activities, but only for the Kansas site (βs: KS = .25, *p* < .05; MA = −.02, *ns*). By contrast, participants who watched a lot of entertainment programs in their teen years participated in fewer service and leadership activities than did less frequent viewers. There was no relation of viewing such programs to academic activities.

Sports Television

For athletic activities, we tested a model that contained sports television and all other television as two predictors. The results of the regressions are shown in Table 32. Adolescents who watched a lot of sports on television participated in more athletic activities than did those who watched

TABLE 32

STANDARDIZED REGRESSIONS FOR ATHLETIC ACTIVITIES AS A FUNCTION
OF VIEWING SPORTS AND NONSPORTS PROGRAMS

	Both Sexes	Males	Females
Background			
Parent education	.13**	.10‡	.16**
Sex	.03	—	—
Birth order	.05	−.02	.10‡
Site	−.01	.05	−.09
Sex × Site	.07	—	—
Time in paid work	−.12**	−.10‡	−.15*
Time in unpaid work	−.06	−.06	−.07
Preschool TV			
Sports	.03	.05	.01
Nonsports	−.02	.002	−.03
Teen TV			
Sports	.28***	.19**	.23***
Nonsports	−.16***	−.16**	−.16**
Interactions			
Sex × Teen Sports TV	−.25*	—	—
Adjusted R^2	.109***	.09***	.13***

‡*p* < .10. *p* < .05. **p* < .01. ***p* < .001.

97

few sports. Although the relation between sports viewing and athletic participation was positive and significant for both sexes, it was slightly more pronounced for females. The interaction of Sex × Sports Television was therefore significant; the βs were male = .09, female = .13. By contrast, teens who engaged in a lot of athletic activities spent *less* time viewing nonsports programs than did those who did not engage in many athletic activities. Preschool sports viewing was unrelated to participation in athletic activities.

CONCLUSIONS

Taken together, the analyses provide no support for the hypothesis that early television viewing fosters a general passivity influencing participation in extracurricular activities during the high school years. There is modest support for hypotheses based on contemporaneous time trade-offs (either displacement or default). Total time watching television was unrelated to the amount of time spent in extracurricular activities, but frequent teen viewers did report fewer activities than infrequent viewers did. In fact, there is more support for the notion that paid work inhibits activity participation, probably because work often occurs during the after-school hours when many teams, clubs, and the like meet. Television, on the other hand, is available at any hour, so it can be watched during time periods that do not overlap with work or outside activities.

The results do support the hypothesis that teens use media and choose activities on the basis of individual interests, motives, and needs. In most instances, viewing informative programs at age 5 predicted participation in academic and service activities, and heavy violence viewing was associated with low participation in leadership activities. In the teen years, those who viewed informative television participated in more academic and service activities, and those who watched violent and other entertainment television participated in fewer leadership activities. It appears that young people with academic interests pursued academic extracurricular activities and watched television programs that provided education and information. Teens with athletic interests and skills spent time in athletic extracurricular activities, and they selected media content about sports.

This conclusion does not imply that media have no effects. The fact that preschool viewing predicted high school participation suggests that patterns of interest may begin early and may be enhanced or maintained in part by television programs. In the teen years, a person may elect to watch certain television programs because of individual interests and preferences, and exposure to those programs may in turn lead to knowledge, attitude changes or additional interests.

SUMMARY

Total amount of viewing in preschool was not related to participation in extracurricular activities. Total viewing in adolescence was unrelated to the time spent in extracurricular activities, but frequent viewers reported fewer different activities than infrequent viewers did. Participants who viewed informative programs in either preschool or adolescence were more likely to participate in academic and service activities and, for males, in leadership activities. Sports viewers of both sexes were most likely to participate in athletic activities.

VIII. HEALTH BEHAVIORS

In this chapter, we shift our focus to the relations of preschool and adolescent television viewing to health-related behavior. In particular, we are concerned with teen alcohol consumption, tobacco use, and body proportion as an index of obesity.

Television content can, in principle, influence adolescents' consumption of alcohol and tobacco in both positive and negative ways. In early childhood and in adolescence, advertisements that promote these products and shows that portray their use may make drinking alcohol and smoking cigarettes seem acceptable, normal, desirable, and consistent with "grown-up" behavior. Early viewing may prime the young child to be more vulnerable to inducements by peers or by other media to consume these products upon reaching pre- or early adolescence. Adolescent viewing may combine with other influences, especially peer pressure, to lower the threshold for trying and using these substances.

Viewing child informative programming, on the other hand, may help to make children conscious of health and healthy behaviors. This health consciousness may induce the pre- or young adolescent to process more carefully and believe health-related messages from the mass media, schools, or parents. Adult informative programming viewed by adolescents may include information about the negative consequences of alcohol and tobacco consumption that would diminish the likelihood of the adolescent's consuming these products.

The hypotheses about alcohol and tobacco use are all based on television content, but both the content and the medium itself have been suggested as potential influences on eating and, by extension, obesity. The content of commercial children's television frequently promotes the high-calorie and high-fat foods in advertising for snacks, candies, and fast food products. Use of the television medium, on the other hand, is typically sedentary in nature. This has produced the popular image of the "couch potato" based on the hypothesis that watching television not only is physically inactive but also displaces time that would otherwise be spent in more physically active behavior. Secondly, television viewing is often accompanied by "grazing" or continuous munching on snack foods. For a review of these effects, see Dietz and Gortmaker (1985).

REVIEW OF EARLIER RESEARCH

Viewing Television and Using Alcohol and Tobacco

Television advertising is designed to promote product use and has long been known to be effective in doing so (National Science Foundation, 1977). In recognition of the effectiveness of advertising, it has been a matter of public health policy since 1971 to ban television advertising of smoking tobacco in the United States. By contrast, beer and wine are heavily advertised on general-audience television. According to Strasburger (1989), American children and teens are exposed to approximately 1,500 television ads for alcohol products annually. These ads frequently associate alcohol consumption with youthful vigor, companionship, sexual imagery, and physical activity, usually sports participation (see Strasburger, 1995, for a review). Some alcohol ads may be attractive to young children, especially when they feature animals or other nonhuman characters (e.g., Budweiser being sold in advertisements featuring talking frogs). Sports television programming is especially likely to contain beer advertising. We have already reported in Chapter 7 that teen participation in sports is associated with viewing sports on television. Eccles and Barber (1999) found that team sports participation was particularly linked to increased use of alcohol from grade 10 to grade 12, but it is not clear whether sports television viewing played a role in this association.

When the participants in the present study were young children, in the early 1980s, television characters used alcohol so often on television that a public outcry prompted the television industry to develop voluntary guidelines for its reduction (Caucus for Producers, Writers, and Directors, 1983, cited by Strasburger, 1995). Nevertheless, a number of content analyses indicate that alcohol use remains frequent, especially in dramatic series and movies made for television (Strasburger, 1995). A 1991 content analysis of prime-time programming revealed six incidents of drinking per hour (Grube, 1993).

Evidence that television viewing actually has an effect on adolescent alcohol consumption is limited. A number of experimental studies have indicated that alcohol advertisements can influence attitudes toward alcohol (e.g., Grube & Wallack, 1994). There is also correlational evidence that television viewing is associated with alcohol consumption (e.g., Aitken, Eadie, Leathar, McNeill, & Scott, 1988; Atkin, Hocking, & Block, 1984; Robinson, Chen, & Killen, 1998; Tucker, 1985), but Chirco (1990, cited by Comstock & Paik, 1991), using a large national sample, did not find a significant relation.

In the lives of the participants in the present research, cigarettes were not advertised on television. Over the 1980s, the frequency of television characters smoking cigarettes steadily decreased, so that by 1982 only 2% of series stars smoked on television (Breed & DeFoe, 1983). Smoking may be considerably more frequent, however, in movies shown on television (Strasburger, 1995).

We found no studies relating viewing of educational television to alcohol and tobacco consumption. Health messages on entertainment television concerning cigarette smoking and alcohol use can influence attitudes and behavior of children and adolescents, but the overall effectiveness of these campaigns is uncertain (Brown & Walsh-Childers, 1994).

Viewing Television and Obesity

Although television characters are generally thin and fit, most theorists have argued that television viewing increases the incidence of obesity. At the time the participants in the present research were preschoolers, about half of advertisements directed at children were for snack food, fast food, candy, and highly sugared cereals (Gerbner, Morgan, & Signorielli, 1982), and this continued into the 1990s (Center for Science in the Public Interest, 1992; Kunkel & Gantz, 1991). Experimental research indicates, not surprisingly, that children's food preferences can be influenced by exposure to food advertising (e.g., Goldberg, Gorn, & Gibson, 1978; Gorn & Goldberg, 1982).

There is also support for the hypothesis that time spent with television is associated with low levels of physical activity and with obesity. Time spent with television is positively related to caloric intake by children (Taras, Sallis, Patterson, Nader, & Nelson, 1989), is negatively related to activity level in childhood (Dietz, 1993), and is positively related to obesity in prospective longitudinal analyses (e.g., Dietz & Gortmaker, 1985). Not all studies, however, have found this latter relation (Robinson et al., 1993).

HYPOTHESES

In the present research we examine the relations of television viewing at age 5 and in adolescence to adolescent alcohol and tobacco use and to a measure indexing obesity. Content-based theory led to the expectation that exposure to adult entertainment programming would be positively related to alcohol use as a consequence of advertising and modeling and positively related to tobacco use from modeling. Because alcohol is especially likely to be advertised with sports programming, we proposed a positive link between viewing sports and alcohol use. Because there is no advertising of smoking tobacco on television, and because smoking is modeled less than drinking, these content-based hypotheses suggest that the relations between viewing adult entertainment programming and drinking would be greater than the relation of viewing to smoking.

Similarly, exposure to child informative television programming as a preschooler and adult informative programming as an adolescent was expected to be negatively related to alcohol and tobacco use. We reasoned that early informative programming may increase a child's processing of health information and that adult informative television may function to inform the adolescent about the negative consequences of alcohol and tobacco use.

With respect to obesity, both content and medium hypotheses led to the prediction that that preschool and adolescent time spent with television would be positively related to BMI, the ratio of weight to height.

METHOD

Alcohol and Tobacco Use

The items assessing alcohol and tobacco use were limited to beer and wine consumption (because these items were advertised on television) and cigarette consumption. Participants were asked whether they ever drink alcohol, and, if so, during how many days in the last month they drank. They were asked parallel questions about smoking.

Body Mass

Participants were asked for their height and weight. From their responses, the Quetelet body mass index (BMI) was calculated as weight in kilograms divided by height in meters squared (Garrow & Webster, 1985).

RESULTS

Adolescent Alcohol Use

More Massachusetts than Kansas participants reported ever drinking beer or wine (61.9% versus 38.1%), and Massachusetts participants reported drinking on more days than Kansas participants (3.87 versus 3.04). These differences probably occurred because Massachusetts participants were on average older than Kansas participants, and many were in the first year of college. About half of both sexes reported ever drinking

103

(males = 51.6% versus females = 48.4%). Of those who ever drank, males drank on more days in a month than did females (4.36 versus 2.70). An analysis of covariance including age as a covariate indicated that the site difference in days of drinking was not significant, although the sex difference was significant, $F(1,334) = 18.38$, $p < .001$. The age covariate was strongly related to days of drinking, $\beta = .92$, $t(334) = 3.31$, $p < .001$.

Because there were no hypotheses about overall television effects on alcohol or tobacco use, the analyses focused on the viewing categories of theoretical interest: preschool exposure to adult entertainment programs, preschool exposure to child informative programs, adolescent exposure to adult entertainment programs, and adolescent exposure to adult informative programs. The analyses did not include "other" viewing or total viewing as predictors.

Because 40.5% of the participants said they never drank, the initial analyses predicted, by means of logistic regression, whether or not the participant drank. There were no main effects of viewing, but there was a significant interaction of sex with adolescent exposure to adult entertainment programs. The analyses were repeated for females and males separately. For females, adolescent viewing of adult entertainment television predicted a low likelihood of drinking (odds ratio = .40, $p < .05$). Odds ratios less than one indicate a negative relation to the dependent variable. For boys, the relation was in the opposite direction (odds ratio = 1.42) but was not significant. Contrary to expectation, then, the more adolescent girls watched adult entertainment television, the less likely they were to drink alcohol.

In a separate analysis we examined the role of viewing sports on television in predicting whether or not a participant drank. In this set of logistic analyses we included as a predictor the number of sports in which the participant reported involvement as a teen (67.9% of the boys and 61.1% of the girls reported involvement with one or more sports, with the maximum number of sports being five). Because the analyses indicated interactions with site, they were performed separately for each site. For the Kansas participants, the relations of drinking with participation in athletics or with sports viewing did not approach significance. For the Massachusetts participants, who were older, involvement in sports marginally predicted drinking (odds ratio = 1.25, $p = .058$) and 5-year-old sports viewing marginally predicted not drinking (odds ratio = .37, $p = .067$). Teen sports viewing was not significantly related to drinking.

The number of days of drinking produced a highly skewed distribution; this variable was transformed as the square root of (the number of days plus one). Transformed days of drinking were regressed on viewing with the usual controls, both with and without participants who reported no drinking. None of these analyses revealed significant effects of interest involving preschool or adolescent viewing of informative, adult entertainment, or sports programming.

Adolescent Cigarette Use

Overall, 28.9% of the participants reported that they had smoked (males = 31.0%; females = 26.9%; Massachusetts = 30.7%; Kansas = 27.0%). The males who smoked reported having smoked an average of 13.6 days in the previous month, and females reported having smoked an average of 12.8 days. Massachusetts smokers reported having smoked an average of 16.3 days in the prior month, whereas Kansas smokers reported having smoked 9.3 days. A Site × Sex analysis of covariance with age at time of interview as the covariate revealed a significant site difference, $F(1,160) = 7.32$, $p < .01$. The age covariate was not significantly related to days of smoking.

Whether or not a participant smoked was analyzed by logistic regression in relation to preschool viewing of child informative and adult entertainment programming and to teen viewing of adult informative and adult entertainment programming. In no case was preschool viewing associated with smoking. Teen viewing of adult informative programming, however, was significantly and negatively associated with smoking (odds ratio = .70, $p < .05$). Of the 84% of participants who reported watching less than 1 hr of adult informative programming a week, 30.9% were smokers; of those who watched 1 hr or more, 18.7% were smokers.

Analysis of the number of days of smoking in the previous month excluded the two thirds of participants who did not smoke. The dependent variable, number of days smoking in the last month, was skewed and was accordingly transformed as square root of (the number of days plus one). The only viewing variable that was significantly related to the outcome variable in the context of controls was preschool viewing of adult entertainment programming ($\beta = -.18$, $p < .05$, adjusted $R^2 = .127$, $p < .001$). In contrast to predictions, the relation was negative. The more adult entertainment programming viewed as a preschooler, the fewer days these smokers smoked.

Adolescent Body Mass

Body Mass Index

A Site × Sex analysis of covariance with participant age at the time of the interview as the covariate indicated that male participants had a larger BMI than females (23.43 versus 21.56), $F(1,560) = 42.56$, $p < .001$. Age was associated with a larger BMI, $\beta = .381$, $p < .05$.

Because most hypotheses relating television viewing to obesity are based on total viewing time, analyses regressed BMI on total preschool viewing time and total teen viewing time. Analyses were conducted separately for males and females. Preschool viewing was not associated with BMI for either sex. Teen viewing, on the other hand, was positively associated with BMI for females, but there was an interaction with site. Because the Kansas participants were younger, this analysis was repeated using age at time of interview as an additional control; the same effects were obtained. Accordingly, the analysis was repeated for the Massachusetts and Kansas girls separately. Although there was a positive association of viewing with BMI in both samples of female participants, the relation was significant only for the Massachusetts participants (β = .35, $p < .01$, adjusted R^2 = .12, $p < .001$).

Obesity

Prior research (e.g., Dietz & Gortmaker, 1985) classified research participants as obese according to a cutoff criterion. Accordingly, we classified the present research participants as obese if their BMI was greater than 25. This criterion was exceeded by more males than females (27.7% versus 11.8%), $\chi^2(1, N = 565) = 23.14$, $p < .001$. Using logistic regression, we examined the relation of preschool and adolescent television viewing to this criterion of obesity. There were no significant relations to television viewing for males. For females there was a significant relation for viewing during adolescence (odds ratio = 1.98, $p < .01$).

CONCLUSIONS

On the basis of the content of television advertising and programs, we expected that adult entertainment viewing would be positively related to alcohol use and that viewing informative programs would predict low use of alcohol. The findings provided no support for this hypothesis; instead we found a small negative relation for female teen viewing. Two possibilities may explain this unanticipated finding. The first is that teenage girls who watch a substantial amount of television spend more of their free time at home and consequently are less likely to be in peer group situations in which teen alcohol use occurs (also see Larson et al., 1989). The second possibility, although less probable in our view, is that during the 1990s alcohol use by television characters was portrayed in a more negative fashion than in earlier times. Strasburger (1995), for example, notes that television dramas in the 1990s became more likely to associate alcohol use with the problems of alcoholism. It is possible that teen females absorbed this message from adult entertainment programming, perhaps especially from daytime soap operas.

Cigarette use was unrelated to teen viewing of adult entertainment programming, a finding that is consistent with the absence of cigarettes in advertising and in most programs. Frequent viewers of adult informative programming were substantially less likely to smoke than were infrequent viewers of informative programming. It is our impression that news and documentaries concerning health issues have treated cigarette smoking in a uniformly negative fashion. The coverage has emphasized the evidence that cigarette smoking causes heart and lung disease, cancer, and wrinkles, among other problems. In contrast, the coverage of alcohol has been less negative, with some emphasis being given to possible health benefits of moderate alcohol consumption. If our participants were influenced by this differing coverage, it is not surprising that there was a greater impact of news and documentaries on cigarette smoking than on alcohol consumption.

Based on the sedentary nature of television viewing, on the practice of continuous grazing while watching television, and on the frequent advertising of high-calorie food products, we predicted a positive association of total television viewing and BMI. The prediction was supported for female teens but not for males. It should be noted that prior research that has found the relation for both sexes has used national samples more than an order of magnitude larger than those available in the present research (Dietz & Gortmaker, 1985). Such large samples allow detection of much smaller statistical associations than is possible in the present work. Although the association of viewing with body mass is consistent with predictions derived from effects of viewing, it is also possible that girls who are overweight are less popular and more likely to spend time at home and consequently watch television more than slimmer girls do.

The relations of viewing to health behavior were observed only for teen viewing. Preschool television viewing was largely unrelated to teen health behaviors, suggesting that any relations between viewing and behavior are not a result of long-term learning or habits established in the early years of life.

SUMMARY

Preschool viewing patterns had no consistent relations to adolescent use of alcohol or tobacco or to body mass. There were few relations of teen viewing to alcohol or tobacco use. Females who often viewed adult entertainment programs were less likely to drink than were less frequent viewers. Teens who viewed informative programs were less apt to smoke than were less frequent viewers. For females, the total amount of television viewed as a teen was associated with a high BMI and with the probability of being obese.

IX. SELF-IMAGE: ROLE MODEL PREFERENCE AND BODY IMAGE

In this chapter, we consider relations of media exposure to two aspects of adolescents' self-image: role model choices and body image. Role models are one source through which children and adolescents acquire attitudes, values, and patterns of conduct. Mass media offer a host of potential models who appear to be attractive, powerful, and glamorous. As children become independent of parents in adolescence, both real and fictional people shown in the mass media may become increasingly important as sources of values and behavior to emulate.

An adolescent who believes that people in the media represent ideals of appearance, behavior, or lifestyle may not only identify with these media figures but also compare him- or herself to them. Two partly conflicting processes may result: efforts to be more like a media role model and increased awareness of the discrepancy between self and model. Social comparison processes could lead to dissatisfaction with oneself.

Body image is one domain in which negative effects of social comparison appear likely to occur. Many adolescents are intensely concerned with bodily characteristics and physical attractiveness, and the media are filled with people who exemplify a cultural ideal of beauty that is difficult for most ordinary adolescents to attain. For females, a critical part of this standard is being thin. In recent years, theorists and social commentators have argued that girls, in particular, are vulnerable to negative self-perceptions and eating disorders as a result of cultural messages that define attractiveness as "thin" (Pipher, 1994). Men, too, can suffer from body dissatisfaction, but they are more likely than women are to be concerned with being too thin or too small. Therefore, in this chapter, we examine adolescents' role models and their satisfaction or dissatisfaction with their height, weight, and physical appearance.

REVIEW OF EARLIER RESEARCH

Media Portrayals of Ideal People

Both observational learning and cultivation theories (see Chapter 1) lead to the proposition that young people will accept the ideals portrayed in the media as indicators of the values in the wider world. The world of entertainment television is populated by physically attractive, affluent people. The men are predominantly young or middle-aged, and the women are predominantly young and thin. Overweight men are two to five times more likely to appear on television than overweight women (Kaufman, 1980; Signorielli, 1993; Silverstein, Peterson, & Perdue, 1986). In one study, female characters on the favorite television shows and music videos of middle school girls were thinner than the average American woman (Gonzalez-Lavin & Smolak, 1995). Even news commentators and anchors appear to be selected partly for physical attractiveness (Signorielli, 1993).

Role Model Choices

As children move from early childhood to adolescence, their choices of role models expand beyond parents, often to media figures (Campbell, 1962). In a 1988 survey, 66% of 12- and 15-year-old children chose glamorous adults (e.g., models, pop stars, and film stars) as their role models, and 8% chose parents and parent surrogates (Duck, 1990, 1992). Because children do not have much experience with the real world, television can often serve as an "early window" on the world. Moreover, those who believe that television is an accurate representation of reality are more likely to identify with its characters and subsequently to choose these media figures as role models (Potter, 1986).

Sex Differences

A child's perception of similarity between him- or herself and the media figure can serve as a basis for identification, and both boys and girls tend to choose same-sex role models. When opposite-sex models are chosen, however, girls do so more frequently than do boys, probably because boys tend to be more rigidly sex-typed than are girls (Duck, 1990; Hoffner, 1996; Huston, 1983; Signorielli, 1993). Girls also chose media figures less often than did boys in surveys of young teens (Duck, 1990). One reason may be that there are more males than females on television, and males play a wider range of roles (Signorielli, 1993).

Reasons for Preferences

Children's role model choices may be based partly on their interest in and attraction to the kinds of activities in which characters are engaged. Males are attracted to characters by physical strength, violence, activity, and supernatural powers; their reasons for choosing role models are varied. Females make choices primarily on the basis of physical and interpersonal attractiveness (Hoffner, 1996). This can be illustrated by comments made by girls explaining their choice of models: for example, "because she is very pretty and has a great figure ... she ... probably has lots of boys ... well men ... running after her" (Duck, 1992, p. 9).

Body Image

Television portrays images of thin women and muscular men that are unrealistic, especially for females. For most women, the ideal body type portrayed on television is unattainable; in one analysis, only 5% of women in a normal weight distribution approximate the media ideal (Kilbourne, 1994). Many of the women who comprise the remaining 95% of the population may devalue their appearance, and there is evidence that adolescent women with high BMIs have low general feelings of self-worth and self-ratings of romantic competence (Mendelson, Mendelson, & Andrews, 2000).

Although commentators assert that media images cause adolescent girls' body dissatisfaction (Fallon, 1990; Thompson & Heinberg, 1993), there is little systematic research investigating this hypothesis (Levine & Smolak, 1996; Tiggemann & Pickering, 1996). In one investigation, there was a relation between total television viewing and body dissatisfaction (K. Harrison & Cantor, 1997), and another found a relation for girls who endorsed a thin ideal (Botta, 1999). In two other studies, the hours of comedy, drama, and game shows viewed predicted disordered eating symptoms (Stice, Schupak-Neuberg, Shaw, & Stein, 1994), and frequent viewers of soap or serial programs and movies had high dissatisfaction, whereas those who watched sports had low levels of dissatisfaction (Tiggemann & Pickering, 1996).

Most researchers have assumed that body standards are different and often more realistic for men than for women, but up to 70% of college men in one study were dissatisfied with their bodies, preferring a more muscular ideal (Tucker, 1982). Unlike females, many adolescent males think they are underweight; hence, their body dissatisfaction is not likely to lead to eating disorders of the kind often seen in females (Kelly, Patten, & Johannes, 1982; Moore, 1990). During the 1990s, an increased media emphasis on possessing a muscular build may have pushed the percentage of boys wishing to be heavier even higher (Drewnowski, Kurth, & Krahn, 1995), potentially pushing boys toward abuse of steroid medications as a way to build muscle mass. None of these studies addressed the relations of mass media exposure to body dissatisfaction.

HYPOTHESES

Content-based theories provide the only clear predictions for role model choice and body image. We expected that the content of television viewed would be related to the type of role model chosen. For example, adolescents who watched a lot of entertainment television were expected to choose media figures as role models; sports television consumers were expected to name sports figures; and those who used informative television were expected to select public figures as role models.

We tested the prediction that exposure to entertainment media would predict body dissatisfaction, particularly for females. Although physical beauty is salient in many types of television, most content analyses indicate that the messages about glamorous body characteristics particularly pervade entertainment television. Therefore, the major categories of viewing used in these analyses were preschool and teen viewing of entertainment television. Sports media were examined separately because they emphasize physical capability and strength. Finally, we examined role model choices as mediators of the relations between media use and body image.

MEASURES

Role Models

Respondents were asked to list up to three persons "whom they would most like to be like." Responses were coded for gender and type of person: parent, other adults known personally (sibling, peer, other adult, grandparent, other relative), sports star, media figure (pop music star; television or movie actor; fictional character from television, movies, or books; model; television personality), real public figure (e.g., Hillary Clinton, Gandhi, Jesus), other, composite of more than one person or qualities of several people, and no one/myself. Respondents gave different numbers of responses, ranging from zero to three, so two scores were created: the category into which the first choice fell, and the proportion of choices in each category (excluding individuals who named no one).

111

Body Image

Height Dissatisfaction

Respondents were asked for their actual and ideal height and weight. Height dissatisfaction was calculated as a proportion by which the ideal height differed from the actual height. The absolute difference between ideal height and actual height was divided by the actual height. A score of zero indicated that the person was satisfied with his or her height.

Weight Dissatisfaction

Weight dissatisfaction was calculated using the same procedure for ideal and actual weight.

Perceived Physical Appearance

The Physical Appearance subtest from the Self-Perception Profile for Adolescents (Harter, 1988) was administered. There are five items, each rated on a 4-point scale. A higher score indicates greater satisfaction with one's appearance. The alpha for the study sample was .74.

RESULTS

Role Models

The first role model choice for 43% of the respondents was a parent or another adult they knew personally. Media figures were named first by 17%, sports stars by 12%, and public figures by 9%. There were no significant differences by age, but males named sports stars more often than females did (19% vs. 5%).

There was a clear pattern of same-sex role model choices. The first person named was the same sex as the respondent for 97% of the males and 85% of the females. When all three choices were considered, 96% of males' choices and 80% of females' choices were of the same sex.

Media Content as a Predictor of Role Model Choices

We expected that the content of the television viewed would be related to the type of role model chosen. Three types of television and corresponding role models were examined: entertainment television as a predictor of selecting media figures as role models, sports television as a predictor of selecting sports figures, and informative television as a predictor of selecting public figures. Because sex is central to role model choices, all analyses were done separately for males and females. There were no significant relations between entertainment viewing and choosing media role models for males or females.

Males who watched a lot of sports television as teens chose more sports figures as role models than did less frequent viewers, $\beta = .25$, $p < .001$, adjusted $R^2 = .112$, $p < .001$. For females, sports viewing during the preschool or teen years was not related to choosing a sports role model.

In the analyses of public figure role model choice, for males, there was an interaction of preschool Informative Viewing × Site, $\beta = -.45$, $p < .05$, $R^2 = .035$, $p < .05$. Separate analyses for the two sites indicated that, for Massachusetts boys, higher viewers of child informative programming chose more public figure role models than lower viewers did, $\beta = .20$, $p < .05$, $R^2 = .048$, $p < .05$. Teen viewing did not predict public figure role model choice, and no viewing categories predicted such choice for females.

Body Image

About equal percentages of males and females were dissatisfied with their height (63% of the males and 61% of the females). Of those who were dissatisfied, slightly over half wanted to be taller (58% of the males and 55% of the females). The majority of the participants were dissatisfied with their weight (72% of males and 75% of females). Of the males, 49% wanted to gain weight, and 23% wanted to lose weight. Of the females, 6% wanted to gain, and 69% wanted to lose weight. The mean physical appearance score for boys was 12.4 ($SD = 2.12$); for girls, it was 12.5 ($SD = 1.91$).

Exposure to Media and Body Image

Entertainment Television

Exposure to entertainment television was expected to predict body dissatisfaction because of the emphasis on glamorous, muscular men and slim, beautiful women. The results of the analyses appear in Table 33. For males, exposure to entertainment television predicted dissatisfaction with height and negative perceptions of physical appearance. Females who watched a lot of entertainment television in the teen years were more apt to be dissatisfied with their weight than were those who watched less entertainment television. An interaction of Television × Site indicated that the relation was stronger for Massachusetts females than for those in Kansas (see Table 33).

113

TABLE 33
SUMMARY OF REGRESSION ANALYSES PREDICTING BODY IMAGE VARIABLES FROM ENTERTAINMENT TELEVISION VIEWING

	Male			Female				
	Dissatisfaction height	Dissatisfaction weight	Perceived appearance	Dissatisfaction height	Dissatisfaction weight			Perceived appearance
					Both sites	KS	MA	
Background								
Parent education	-.02	-.03	.03	.02	-.02	.07	-.08	-.07
Birth order	.02	.04	.09	-.06	-.02	-.03	-.01	.17**
Site (MA)	-.21**	-.13*	-.01	-.09	-1.10*	—	—	.04
Preschool TV								
Informative	.04	.00	.00	-.06	.01	-.11	.14	-.08
Entertainment	-.11	.07	-.04	.00	-.02	.01	-.04	.00
Teen TV								
Informative	.06	.01	.09	-.01	-.01	.05	-.05	.03
Entertainment	.15*	.08	-.21**	.11‡	.29***	.19‡	.37***	.00
Interactions								
Site × Preschool Informative	—	—	—	—	-.37‡	—	—	—
Site × Teen Entertainment	—	—	—	—	-1.00*	—	—	—
Adjusted R^2	.036*	.016	.042**	-.004	.102***	-.004	.144***	.027*

‡$p < .10$. *$p < .05$. **$p < .01$. ***$p < .001$.

Sports Television

Viewing sports television could be associated with positive body images if it reflects athletic interests and involvement. On the other hand, it could lead to unfavorable social comparisons with the star athletes featured on television. Regressions of body image on sports television viewing demonstrated that, for males, teen sports television viewing was associated with dissatisfaction with height, $\beta = .25$, $p < .001$, adjusted $R^2 = .112$, $p < .001$, and negative perceptions of physical appearance, $\beta = -.18$, $p < .05$, adjusted $R^2 = .044$, $p < .05$. Seventy-eight percent of females ($n = 220$) reported no sports television viewing at the teen interview; sports viewing did not predict body image for females.

Role modeling might be one means by which television viewing affects body image. We examined this possibility using the methods outlined by Baron and Kenny (1986). In order for a variable (e.g., role model choice) to be a mediator, it has to be predicted by the television category, and it has to predict the outcome (e.g., body image). The only case in which viewing predicted role model choice was the relation of sports viewing to males' choice of sports role models (reported above). Choosing a sports role model significantly predicted males' dissatisfaction with height ($\beta = .13$, $p < .05$, $t = 2.234$) but not perceived physical appearance. The relation of viewing to height dissatisfaction was not substantially reduced, however, when sports role model choice was added to the model ($\beta = .18$, $p < .05$, $t = 2.55$). Therefore, there was no support for the hypothesis that role models mediated the relations of viewing to height dissatisfaction, weight dissatisfaction, or perceived physical appearance for either sex.

CONCLUSIONS

The major purpose of these analyses was to examine the relations of television use to role model choice and body image. In some respects, the results suggest that adolescents' role model choices are not heavily influenced by exposure to television. Many of the people whom teens named as role models were individuals they knew personally, including parents. Preschool viewing was generally not related to role model choices, and, with the exception of sports, teen exposure to related television content did not predict such choices either.

Nonetheless, almost half of the people named first by males and 35% of those named by females were people from the entertainment media, sports, or public life. The mass media in a broad sense are virtually the only available sources of information about these individuals, so television and other mass media must contribute directly or indirectly to young people's admiration for them.

The contemporaneous associations do not, of course, indicate causal direction. In fact, unidirectional causal explanations are probably overly simplistic. The most reasonable explanation appears to be the hypothesis derived from a uses and gratifications perspective (Rosengren, 1994). Teens who are interested in a topic are likely to select television programs about that topic, and they are likely to admire the people who exemplify excellence in that domain. Television plays a role in providing and shaping the information available about the topic; in that sense, it may influence the perceptions of the adolescent viewer. For example, adolescents may watch sports on television because they enjoy athletics, but the individuals and qualities that are highlighted on television may influence the particular sports heroes that they choose.

We expected that viewing entertainment television (and possibly sports), much of which emphasizes glamour and physical appearance, would lead not only to identification with television figures but also to social comparison with them. The outcomes might well be unfavorable self-comparisons to the extraordinarily attractive and physically fit people who inhabit the world of television. The findings of our analyses were consistent with this hypothesis for both males and females.

Viewing entertainment television negatively predicted body image for both males and females. It appears reasonable to attribute this finding to content rather than to a characteristic of the medium itself, but the distinction is difficult to draw empirically. Content analyses have indicated that physical attractiveness characterizes people shown on television in almost all types of programming, including the news. Hence, the messages about desirable body characteristics are homogeneous across much of the programming viewed by young people.

There were sex differences in the bodily characteristics that were related to television viewing. For males, television viewing, including sports viewing, predicted dissatisfaction with height and general physical appearance. For females, television viewing was most consistently related to dissatisfaction with weight. These differences appear to reflect the ideals for each sex that are portrayed on entertainment television, and, for males, on sports programming as well.

Height, strength, and muscular physique are valued for men in many types of programs. Sports programming generally features tall, muscular players. The focus on height may have been particularly salient because the data were collected between January and June in or near university communities where basketball is a major topic of interest. For boys who identify with sports stars or who have a strong interest in sports, seeing the stars on television may increase the awareness that they have not attained the extraordinary height that is important for success in many sports, but particularly basketball.

Television's ideal body type for women is represented by pervasive images of female fashion models and actresses who are young, tall, long-legged, and very slender (Gordon, 1990; Signorielli, 1993). It is not surprising, therefore, that adolescent girls who watch these images often want to be thinner than they are. The relation of viewing to dissatisfaction with weight may also have been based on objective assessment of body characteristics; females who watched a lot of entertainment television were objectively more overweight than were infrequent viewers (see Chapter 8). Television may play a particularly problematic role for these female teens. As a sedentary activity, television viewing may play a causal role in their obesity. At the same time, television presents them with almost unattainable images of thin glamorous women, thus increasing their dissatisfaction with their own appearance.

Although young women who selected role models from sports media tended to be more satisfied with their weight than other females were, there was no evidence that sports television viewing contributed directly to their satisfaction or dissatisfaction. As noted in Chapter 6, females who participated in sports activities often watched sports television. They were also more likely to choose sports role models ($r = .32$, $p < .001$) and to have a lower BMI ($r = -.13$, $p < .05$). An interest in sports may lead to athletic activity as well as to selection of television programs and role models. This combination may contribute to physical fitness and to satisfaction with one's weight.

The opposite pattern appears to have occurred for males who used sports media. They were apt to name sports role models, to participate in athletics (see Chapter 6), and to express some dissatisfaction with their height. The difference may arise from the fact that height is not as easily altered as weight. A person cannot work out or change his diet to become taller.

The findings are consistent with the hypothesis that seeing beautiful or strong people on television leads to negative social comparisons for teenagers. It is also possible, however, that adolescents who were smaller (for boys), more overweight (for girls), or less physically attractive than others (for both sexes) were less popular and less involved in peer group activities; hence, they might have had more time to watch television. In Chapter 6, we reported that, for both sexes, there was some tendency for those who watched a lot of entertainment programming to participate in fewer extracurricular activities than did infrequent viewers. The fact that males who chose media figures as role models were less satisfied with their height than were other males suggests, however, that the extensive exposure to entertainment television, whatever its origin, may have had some impact on males' perceptions of their physical characteristics.

SUMMARY

About 38% of the respondents named a media, sports, or public figure as their first choice of role model, but role model choices were predicted by the content of television programs viewed in only one of six comparisons. For males, watching sports television predicted choosing a sports star as a role model, but there were no relations for either sex between watching entertainment programs and choosing media role models or between watching informative programs and choosing public figures as role models.

Males who watched a lot of entertainment television or a lot of sports television were less satisfied with their height and physical appearance than were males who did not watch a lot of entertainment television. Females who watched a lot of entertainment television were more dissatisfied with their height and particularly with their weight than were infrequent viewers. Females who chose sports role models were more satisfied with their weight, but sports viewing did not predict females' body images.

X. SUMMARY AND CONCLUSIONS

This study evaluated adolescents who had been in either of two comparable studies as 5-year-olds during the early 1980s and who were aged 15 to 18 when we recontacted them for a long interview and official high school transcripts. Both original samples were convenience samples in which ethnic minorities were underrepresented and middle- and working-class Caucasians were overrepresented. Multiple regressions were the major form of analysis, and most of these regressions were used to predict self-reported teen television use, school achievement, self-image, creativity, body image, leisure reading, and health behaviors, along with accompanying attitudes and motivation. The predictors were mostly data on television use by categories of program viewing taken from week-long diaries of television programs watched by the children as preschoolers 10 or so years earlier. Recall that in these regressions, control variables entered first included mother's years of education, site (Kansas vs. Massachusetts), birth order, and sometimes scores on the PPVT-R administered at age 5.

In this chapter we review the theoretical positions bearing on our analyses and provide an overall summary of the findings, followed by a few important conclusions.

Theories relating television viewing to development fall into two broad categories: those that emphasize the content of what is viewed and those positing effects of television as a medium, irrespective of content. Some of the latter group emphasize effects on use of time and participation in different types of activity; others stress forms and formats, including visual images, pacing, and lack of intellectual challenge. Within each of these broad categories, some theories emphasize the effects of television on viewers; others stress the viewer's role in selecting and using media for particular purposes.

In our analyses of the relations of preschool and concurrent teen viewing to adolescent development, we have tested hypotheses drawn from a wide range of these theories. The results provide much stronger support

TABLE 34

SUMMARY OF SIGNIFICANT FINDINGS BY TELEVISION CATEGORY

Informative Television
High preschool child informative (vs. low) predicts:
• Higher grades (total GPA, English, math and science) (boys).
• Higher leisure time book reading.
• Higher competence beliefs (total, math, science), but the effect is mediated by grades.
• Higher value attached to achievement, especially in math and science (boys).
• Choosing higher-level math courses, with grades, competence beliefs, and task value controlled (boys).
• Tendency to higher ideational fluency (boys).
• Higher participation in creative activities and art classes (KS site).
• Lower aggression (boys).
• Higher participation in service activities.
• Higher participation in academic activities (MA males).
High viewing of *Sesame Street* (vs. low) predicts:
• Higher grades in science.
• Higher grades (total GPA, English) (boys).
• Higher leisure-time book use.
• More participation in art classes (KS girls).
• Lower aggression (boys).
High *Mister Rogers' Neighborhood* viewing (vs. low) predicts:
• Higher ideational fluency.
• Higher participation in creative activities (KS site).
High teen viewing of informative programs (vs. low) predicts:
• Participation in more creative activities (KS site).
• Participation in more service extracurricular activities.
• Participation in more academic extracurricular activities (girls).
• Lower likelihood of smoking.
Violent Television
High preschool violence viewing (vs. low) predicts:
• Lower grades (total GPA and English, math and science) (girls).
• Higher math competence beliefs, with GPA controlled (overestimation).
• Higher English competence beliefs with GPA controlled (girls).
• Participation in fewer creative activities (KS site) and art classes.
• Higher aggression (KS girls; and boys and girls who were moderately or highly focused on television as preschool children).
• Participation in fewer leadership activities.
• Participation in fewer academic extracurricular activities (KS girls).
High teen violence viewing (vs. low) predicts:
• Lower grades (total GPA, English, science) (boys and MA girls).
• Higher competence beliefs in science, with grades controlled (overestimation).
• Higher competence beliefs in English, with grades controlled (girls).
• Lower value for math, with grades controlled (girls).
• Higher ideational fluency (girls).
• More art classes (MA site).
• Higher aggression (MA females).
• Lower participation in leadership activities.

(continued)

TABLE 34 – *Continued*

Other Entertainment Television
High preschool viewing (vs. low) predicts:
• Lower math competence beliefs, with grades controlled (underestimation).
• Lower ideational fluency (girls).
• Participation in more leadership activities (KS site).
• Lower frequency of smoking.
High teen viewing (vs. low) predicts:
• Lower grades in science (boys).
• Lower leisure time book reading.
• Lower academic competence beliefs (total, science), with grades controlled.
• Lower English competence beliefs, with grades controlled (girls).
• Lower ideational fluency (boys).
• Lower participation in leadership and service activities.
• Higher aggression (MA females).
• Lower likelihood of drinking alcohol (girls).
• More dissatisfaction with height and physical appearance (boys).
• More dissatisfaction with weight (girls).
Sports Television
High teen sports television viewing (vs. low) predicts:
• Higher athletic participation.
• Choosing more sports figures as role models (boys).
• More dissatisfaction with height and general physical appearance (boys).
Total Television
High preschool total television viewing (vs. low) predicts:
• Higher average grades (total GPA, English, math, science) (boys).
• Lower average grades (total GPA, science) (girls).
• Higher leisure time book use.
• Lower ideational fluency (girls).
• Taking fewer art classes.
High teen total viewing (vs. low) predicts:
• Higher leisure time book reading (MA females).
• Lower ideational fluency (boys).
• Participation in fewer extracurricular activities.
• Higher body mass (girls).

for content-based hypotheses than for theories emphasizing television as a medium. Content-based hypotheses accounted for our findings in almost all of the behaviors studied.

The chapters of the *Monograph* are organized around the "dependent variables," such as achievement, aggression, and self-image, that many people think are influenced by television. In this summary chapter, we consider each category of preschool television viewing in relation to all adolescent behaviors investigated. The findings for each type of preschool television viewing are summarized in Table 34.

PRESCHOOL MEDIA USE AND ADOLESCENT BEHAVIOR

Preschool Informative Programs

Informative or educational programs watched as young children had different and often opposite relations to intellectual and social behavior of the adolescents than did programs with violent or other types of entertainment content. The positive relations between viewing child informative programs and adolescent behaviors were much more consistent for males than for females, although the same pattern occurred for both sexes. Male viewing of child informative programs in preschool was associated with better grades in English, math, and science in high school, greater perceived competence in these subjects, and greater value placed on achievement. Boys who were among the heaviest viewers of child informative programming also chose to take more advanced math classes, had slightly higher ideational fluency, and had less-aggressive attitudes. For children of both sexes, viewers of child informative programs read more books, as teens, outside of school; had higher perceptions of their academic competence; participated in more creative, service, and academic extracurricular activities; and took more art classes than did infrequent viewers. All of these associations held true after taking into account family background, other categories of preschool viewing, and adolescent media use.

This pattern is consistent with the early learning model, which proposes a straightforward process by which children learn content from television through observation and participation. Further support for the model is provided by separate analyses of preschool viewing of *Sesame Street* and *Mister Rogers' Neighborhood* (as these programs were the most prominent children's educational programs between 1979 and 1983). Content analyses in the early 1990s demonstrated that *Sesame Street* was one of the few educational programs with emphasis on cognitive and language skills (Neapolitan & Huston, 1994). *Mister Rogers' Neighborhood,* on the other hand, placed strong emphasis on fantasy, pretending, and activities that might be expected to promote creativity. The differing findings with respect to these particular programs are consistent with their differences in content.

Adolescents' academic grades and the amount of leisure reading they did were related specifically to how much they watched *Sesame Street* as preschoolers, and not, for the most part, to viewing other informative programs at either time period. In addition, early *Sesame Street* viewing positively predicted some academic behaviors (for example, science grades and leisure time book use) for girls as well as for boys. Creativity, on the other hand, was predicted most consistently by viewing *Mister Rogers' Neighborhood.*

If early viewing affects high school achievement and behavior, then by what pathways might that influence occur? Our analyses do not suggest that teens' current viewing patterns mediated the effects of pre-school viewing. That is, it does not appear that viewing educational programming in preschool leads to a continuing pattern of viewing infor-mative programs, which in turn lasts until adolescence, where it has con-current influence on achievement or other behaviors, though such may be a minor path of influence. Such early viewing could have started a pattern of viewing educational television that lasted through childhood and contributed to adolescent learning efficacy. The problem is that while there were a few good programs for kids at the preschool level, there were very few educational programs directed to children in middle child-hood in the early 1990s. Since then a proliferation of such programming has emerged with the broadcasters' response to the FCC's "3-hour rule." But the programming necessary to support a habit of viewing or a "continuity-of-viewing" explanation, though present today, was not avail-able to this cohort in middle to late childhood.

Instead, it seems likely that early viewing sets in motion a chain of events that affects children's developmental trajectories in the critical early years of formal schooling. Three facets of early development are impli-cated as pathways through which long-term consequences of educational media may occur. These are learning preacademic skills, particularly in reading and language; developing motivation and interest in education; and learning control of aggression. Our findings show a relation of edu-cational viewing to these domains in adolescence. Differences in these characteristics when children enter school are likely to be magnified over time because they set children on different developmental trajectories of school achievement, and because they lead children to select and seek different opportunities for learning. We know that preschool viewing of educational programs is related to school readiness at entry (Wright et al., in press). Children with good academic skills, motivation, and behavioral self-control are likely to be placed in higher ability groups from the very beginning, to be perceived by teachers as better students, and to succeed in the early school years (Entwisle et al., 1997). They may also be more likely to seek out and voluntarily participate in activities such as reading and playing educational games (Huston et al., 1999). These pathways are similar to those proposed by Barnett (1995) for long-term influences of other early childhood educational interventions.

Preschool Viewing of Violent Programs

Content-based theories lead to the direct prediction that viewing vio-lence in the preschool years is associated with increased aggression. More indirect effects, negative ones, on school achievement are predicted as a result of the known direct effects of violent content on children's ability

123

to control their behavior. Our findings provide modest support for the prediction that viewing violence leads to increased aggression, but only for particular subgroups of children. We also find some support for the prediction that viewing of violent programs has indirect negative effects on school achievement and creativity.

Our findings were consistent with earlier studies showing that children who identify with television characters are most likely to be influenced by television violence (Huesmann & Eron, 1986). Our preschool measure of such identification was television focus, which measured how often the child used television characters and themes in play and conversation. When children of both sexes were very involved with television as preschoolers, the more violence they viewed, the more aggressive they were as adolescents. For children with low involvement with television, there was no relation between viewing violence and aggression, suggesting that individual differences in degree of engagement may lead to different levels of susceptibility to television effects, at least for aggression. Among young children for whom television generally played a central role in fantasy and conversation, the violent content of what they viewed made more difference in later aggression than it did for children whose play and conversation was not focused on television. Television focus, however, did not moderate the observed negative relation between early exposure to violent television and subsequent academic achievement.

Children who viewed a great deal of violence in preschool continued to be heavy viewers in adolescence, so the relations of preschool violence viewing to adolescent aggression could be a result of long-term exposure. In our analyses, teen viewing levels mediated preschool viewing effects for one subgroup, those with moderate levels of childhood television focus, but not for the subgroup with high levels of childhood television focus. Most theories would predict cumulative effects of viewing over childhood and adolescence, but the findings for the high television focus group are consistent with Huesmann and Miller's (1994) proposal that viewing in childhood has a stronger association than later viewing with young adult behavior.

The findings also provide some support for indirect effects of viewing violence on school achievement and creativity, particularly for girls. Girls who were heavy preschool viewers of violent programs had lower grades and attached less value to science than did light viewers. Nonetheless, they evaluated their academic competence more favorably, suggesting greater academic confidence or perhaps assertiveness. Preschool violence viewing was related to low participation in creative and leadership activities and in art classes in high school.

These findings should be interpreted in the light of our imperfect index of violent television. It is certainly true that cartoons and action-adventure programs have considerably higher rates of violence than other program types do (Gerbner et al., 1994), but not all are violent, and other programs also show violence. This limitation may have added error that reduced the power of our analysis to detect relations and may thus have contributed to our failure to find a general relation of violence viewing to teen aggression, as has been found in other studies. From another perspective, however, cartoons, which constituted the majority of the violent programs that preschoolers watched, have formal features that could also contribute to aggression, reduced imaginative play, and low behavior control (Huston & Wright, 1989). It is difficult, if not impossible, to disaggregate the violent content from the high levels of action, visual gimmicks, sound effects, and rapid pace that characterized the majority of cartoons shown in the early 1980s (Huston et al., 1981).

Other Entertainment Programs

By definition, the content of entertainment programs that is neither informative nor violent is highly varied. Hence, content theories cannot be used to induce specific predictions relating content to behavior, and, indeed, there were only scattered relations of such viewing to academic and intellectual behaviors.

We tested one specific hypothesis based on the content of adult commercial entertainment programs and advertising. Because smoking was rarely shown on television, whereas alcohol was portrayed often in both advertising and programs, we predicted that early viewing would not be associated with smoking but would be linked to drinking. In fact, children who watched a lot of entertainment programs in preschool were *less* likely than infrequent viewers to smoke in adolescence, and there was no relation of viewing to drinking alcohol. As we have no direct evidence of antismoking messages on television viewed by our participants, this result is not necessarily a response to content viewed, though it well may be so.

Total Time With Television in Childhood

Theories positing long-term effects of the medium of television, irrespective of its content, received little support from this study. The few instances in which total television viewing in the preschool years was related to teen behavior (see Table 34) are explained by the further analyses of program content. Contrary to the predictions of most total-exposure theories, boys who watched a lot of television at age 5 had better high school grades than those who watched little, but the difference was entirely due to viewing child informative programs, not to viewing general

125

entertainment programming. Similarly, girls who watched little television in the preschool years had better grades and higher ideational fluency scores than heavy viewers, but the difference was due to watching fewer violent and general entertainment programs, not to viewing fewer children's informative programs.

Television Form

Two theories provided specific hypotheses about the negative impact of television form. Our data flatly contradicted both. Healy (1990) proposed that the visual nature of television is inimical to language development; hence, even programs designed to be educational would reduce language acquisition, resulting in poorer school performance. J. L. Singer (1980) proposed that the rapid pace and disconnected segments of *Sesame Street* would lead to superficial processing and low attention span, both of which would interfere with school performance and make it less likely that children would elect reading as an activity.

The findings showed quite the opposite—that viewing children's informative programs, especially *Sesame Street*, was associated with higher levels of school performance in English, math, and science. Moreover, teens who had watched educational programs, particularly *Sesame Street*, were considerably more likely to read books that were not required for school than were their peers who had been infrequent viewers of *Sesame Street* as preschoolers.

Causal Direction, Methodological Limitations, and Alternative Explanations

Our finding that preschool television use has discernible relations to high school grades and other teen behaviors is, we think, impressive. Most of the patterns are consistent with theories positing effects of television content on development, and the long time period between media exposure and predicted behavior suggests a causal role for television. That said, there are methodological limitations of this research that should be acknowledged.

Our sample, from two regionally distinct communities, is a White, working- to middle-class sample of largely intact families in which at least one parent is employed. Even within these descriptors, the original sample was not randomly drawn based on demographics of the two communities or of the nation at large. As in any research based on convenience samples, there will always be some limitation on how general the results might be with respect to other populations.

As in any study involving multiple measures, some measures are better than others. For example, although we are quite confident that the preschool viewing diaries are valid and reliable measures of viewing, our measures of teen viewing, based on a single telephone interview and questioning "typical" viewing, are likely less so. Similarly, our measure of aggression, based on a subset of items in the original instrument, may have limited our ability to find a general relation across both sites between preschool viewing and teen aggression. Alternatively, however, our measure of adolescent aggression is a self-report of tendencies to carry out many forms of aggression, including irritability, verbal aggression, and indirect aggression, as well as physical attack. Because it includes many forms of "ordinary" aggressive behavior, it may detect individual differences within the normal range better than do measures focusing solely on physical or deviant aggression. Nevertheless, the study is certainly open to the criticism that, where we failed to find an expected relation, if we had used a better measure, the relation might have been found.

Even a longitudinal study is correlational, and we cannot exclude the possibility that those individual or family differences among children that affected their choice of television at age 5 were the same ones that affected later teen behavior. Our controls for sex, site, parent education, and birth order eliminated some of the potential selection effects, but there is always the possibility that unmeasured variables influenced both early viewing and teen behavior. In particular, we cannot exclude alternative "third-variable" explanations of some plausibility. For example, our academic achievement results might be partially explainable in terms of inherent individual differences in children. It is possible that children drawn to such child informative programs as *Sesame Street* are strongly predisposed to appreciate any kind of learning experiences. Consequently, these children do well in school regardless of their early television viewing. As another possibility, parents who encourage child informative viewing may be the same parents who encourage academic achievement. Adjusting the regression equations for parents' education probably only partially controls for this possibility. From this perspective, child informative viewing may be an early marker for later academic achievement but is not conclusively a primary cause. Hence, although our findings are consistent with the idea that early television content plays a causal role in teen behavior and attitude, the findings also come with a strong caution about concluding that these are simple causal effects of early viewing.

Perhaps more important, most sophisticated conceptualizations of the role of media in children's development (e.g., Neuman, 1995) reject a simplistic unidirectional model. It is more likely that individual characteristics of children and their environment affect viewing choices *and* that the programs, in turn, influence the learning, behavior, and attitudes of the children. Moreover, differences in personality, interests, and abilities may lead different children to absorb and remember different messages

127

and information from the same program. Within this model, associations between early viewing patterns and later behaviors reflect both child initiative, which in turn is influenced by the child's environment, and effects of viewing particular kinds of programming.

Preschool television viewing cannot realistically be considered a proximal cause of the major adolescent behavioral variables. For example, nothing in *Sesame Street* is likely to be the subject of high school tests, so the content of *Sesame Street* can play only a distal role in relation to high school grades. Consequently, we did not expect, nor did we obtain, large effect sizes for preschool viewing on teenage behaviors. Almost certainly, moreover, not all effects observed are unidirectional. It is likely that later viewing is influenced by early personal characteristics like intelligence, and by family structure, as well as by early viewing, and it is perhaps even more likely that a string of achievement characteristics and behaviors are instigated in part by an early diet of educational television. Exclusive causality or major attribution of sources of adolescent outcomes is not the point. Rather we emphasize the stable and lasting nature of achievement trajectories that were observed to diverge early and that were expected to be associated with differential early viewing diets.

ADOLESCENT MEDIA USE

A synergistic model for the role of media (Neuman, 1995) is obviously appropriate in understanding the contemporaneous relations of teens' media use to the behaviors and attitudes that we measured. There is no basis in this study for inferring causal direction between teen viewing and contemporaneous achievement, behavior, and attitudes. Instead, our results point to the use of media as part of individuals' ongoing patterns of interests, activities, and skills. As was true for the preschoolers, however, the content of television and other media is critical to understanding teen patterns. Two content-based patterns are suggested: one based on informative media and one on sports. In both cases, it appears that teens use media to pursue their interests and that these interests are in turn served by media. The patterns are summarized in Table 34.

Teens who used informative media evidenced participation and interest in the larger world. They watched documentaries, read the Sunday paper, and participated in several types of extracurricular activities involving service, academic, and creative activities. Among such teens, both sexes were less likely to smoke, perhaps as result of information about health hazards that appears often in news and other informative programming.

Teens who frequently watched sports also participated in athletic activities, read the newspaper, read sports magazines, and chose sports figures as role models. Boys were considerably more involved with sports and sports media than were girls, so some of these patterns occurred exclusively for young men. One finding suggests, however, that viewing sports may have a negative effect on males' self-perception. Boys who were frequent viewers as teens were unsatisfied with their height and physical appearance. Height is a physical characteristic over which a person has little control. The sports shown on television feature exceptional players, often of large physical stature. Accordingly males who are especially interested in sports may compare themselves negatively with the stars.

In adolescence, the majority of programs viewed that we classified as violent were action-adventure shows; teens watched relatively few cartoons. The patterns associated with viewing violence as teens did not suggest strong content-based relations between viewing and aggression. That is, teen viewing of violence was not related to aggression for most of the sample. An exception occurred for girls in Massachusetts, but this pattern is not entirely consistent with content effects, because more-aggressive girls watched both violent and general entertainment programs more than did less-aggressive girls.

Viewing violence as a preschooler was, however, specifically characteristic of adolescents who received low grades. With the exception of males' science grades, the concurrent relations of grades to other types of viewing were not significant. Moreover, frequent preschool viewers of violence were more apt to overestimate their competence, at least in science later on, perhaps indicating greater assertiveness or unrealistic evaluations of their performance, even though the girls among them valued achievement in math less. There was also some tendency for adolescents who viewed a lot of violence to participate less in extracurricular activities involving leadership. The meaning of this pattern is unclear, but it suggests that teens whose viewing diets are heavily weighted with action-adventure may be less identified and involved with school and academic achievement than are those who watch other types of television. At the same time, these teens had unrealistically high assessments of their competence.

The majority of programming viewed by teens was general entertainment, which includes many types of content. It can be argued, however, that much of this fare presents a media culture emphasizing physical appearance, glamour, fun, material possessions, and immediate gratification, with a deemphasis on hard work, achievement, and intellectual values (Signorielli & Morgan, 1990). Our data provide support for the hypothesis that viewing entertainment fare in the adolescent years is associated with low levels of mental effort and involvement in outside activities. Teens who watched a lot of entertainment television had relatively low perceptions of their academic competence, even with grades taken into account, and they were less likely to be involved in leadership and service as extracurricular activities. They also evidenced dissatisfaction with their bodily characteristics and physical appearance, perhaps as a result of unfavorable comparisons with the glamorous people in these media. The boys among them had lower grades in science and lower ideational fluency scores.

The fact that these patterns emerged in relation to viewing entertainment programming (e.g. situation comedies, game shows, and nonviolent drama) and were in many respects different from the correlates of viewing violent or informative programs suggests that they are a function of the characteristics of the programs viewed rather than of television viewing in general. We stress, once again, that causal direction cannot be inferred. Teens who are less able, less involved in activities, less popular and socially active, or unsatisfied with themselves may seek light entertainment programming, and such programming may, in return, demand little thought or activity.

Media Relations to Time Use and Activities

Many theorists propose that contemporaneous relations between television use and other activities result from effects of media on the way people spend their time. Because entertainment constitutes so much of total viewing, it is difficult to separate the effects of time with the medium from those of exposure to its predominant content.

Our findings for teens do support some time trade-offs between television viewing and other activities, though we do not know whether these indicate effects of viewing on activities or consequences of other activity choices for viewing. Adolescents who watched a lot of television participated in fewer extracurricular activities than did less frequent viewers, but they did not report spending less time doing homework. Frequent viewers were also slightly *less* likely to smoke or drink, and girls (but not boys) who watched a lot of entertainment television drank less and were more likely to be overweight than low viewers. One hypothesis explaining these somewhat disparate findings is that teens who watch a lot of television are more closely tied to their home and parents and less involved in peer group activities. They go out less for extracurricular activities, and they may participate less in partying as well. Other time use studies have shown that teens who watch a lot of television tend to do so with their families (Larson et al., 1989).

Effective parental monitoring could have improved the quality of television viewed at age 5 and the study habits in force when the study participants reached adolescence. The statistical controls for parent education represented an attempt to preclude that causal pattern's being mistaken for the learning model's success. However, our early childhood research showed complex correlates of restrictive and encouraging parental management of television use. It appears that parental regulation is sometimes a response to perceived viewing abuses and sometimes the antecedent of temporarily better viewing habits. But these reciprocal processes appear to cycle through alternating phases wherein parents and children influence and respond to each other by turns.

Television viewing is sedentary, and there is evidence from past studies that extensive viewing contributes to obesity and low levels of physical activity (Dietz & Gortmaker, 1985). The one measure relevant to this hypothesis in our study was BMI, an index of weight corrected for height. Girls who watched a lot of television were heavier than those who did not. Frequent viewers were also likely to be dissatisfied with their weight, perhaps because of their greater body mass. This finding is consistent with the hypothesis that viewing promotes weight gain, but it is also possible that girls who are heavy (or who feel that they are) are less popular with peers and less likely to participate in peer group activity. They may thus spend more time at home, where television can be a default activity.

SEX DIFFERENCES

The positive relations of early educational viewing to school achievement, achievement motivation, and aggression were much more pronounced for boys than for girls. This pattern occurred for child informative programs generally and to a lesser extent for *Sesame Street*. One hypothesis is that child informative programs in the early 1980s were differentially appealing to a male audience. For example, *Sesame Street* was criticized because the most attractive characters, such as the Muppets, were predominantly male. To us, this hypothesis is unlikely to account for the effect, because studies in the 1970s and 1980s of preschoolers' attention to and comprehension of *Sesame Street* almost never revealed effects related to the sex of the viewer (Anderson & Field, 1983). Girls appear to learn from and appreciate the program as much as boys do. Boys and girls watch *Sesame Street* and other children's informative programs about equally often at home (Wright & Huston, 1995). Moreover, violent programs were even more male-dominated, and yet girls appeared to be more affected by watching them than boys.

A second hypothesis is that girls are simply better prepared for school than boys and that boys are, conversely, more at risk of initial failure. Interventions are often most effective for groups who are at risk for failure to develop in a domain. In the early years, boys are generally less mature than girls, and they do less well in school throughout childhood and adolescence. Boys more often have both academic and behavior problems

131

in school, and their average levels of aggression are higher than are girls'. Teachers of young children are more likely to be female. In American society, boys are socialized to be active and aggressive, but girls are encouraged to be compliant and responsive to adults (Golombok & Fivush, 1994). As a consequence, boys may benefit more from the academic and prosocial messages provided by educational programs because these messages go against the grain of other socialization influences for boys but not for girls.

If television is likely to have greater effects when it counteracts predominant socialization influences, it is probably no accident that the only statistically significant positive relation between educational preschool viewing and high school grades for girls was the relation of *Sesame Street* viewing to science grades. If our general reasoning is correct that the long-term benefits of early viewing are maximal when other developmental expectations do not support later positive behaviors, then we should expect positive effects for girls in science and perhaps math but not in English. Obtaining that result for science (as well as a marginally positive relation for math when *Sesame Street* viewing is considered separately) supports the general proposition that early viewing has the strongest long-term correlates when it goes against the normative developmental trends for the group in question.

Conversely, the negative relations between exposure to preschool violent programs and school achievement were limited to girls. Unlike educational programs that have about equal appeal to girls and boys, cartoons and action-adventure programs are clearly more appealing to boys than girls. Boys watch more violence at home, and they name violent programs as their favorites more often than girls do. Hence, boys who watch such programs frequently are more "typical" of their sex. Girls who are heavy consumers of cartoon and live violence are less typical of their sex. They may be temperamentally more inclined to activity and aggression, and they may be more susceptible to the effects of exposure to violent programs than girls who rarely choose to watch them. Or the long-term negative effects of those programs may be stronger because their messages go against the developmental trend for girls toward prosocial and self-disciplined behavior.

We do not know whether the sex differences found in this study will generalize to other populations. In their Swedish samples, Rosengren and his associates (Rosengren, Johnsson-Smaragdi, & Sonesson, 1994) also found a negative relation of general television viewing to later academic performance for girls but not for boys. Their result also supports the "against-the-developmental-expectations" hypothesis.

If the positive correlates of viewing for boys generalize to less economically advantaged populations, it would be especially encouraging. The achievement gap between boys and girls for children living in poverty is much larger than the gap for more advantaged children. As a relatively inexpensive societal investment that reaches many children in poor families, educational television may help boys in such families to be better prepared for school. Early success in school can help initiate a cascade of positive outcomes that benefit not only the children themselves, but the society with the wisdom to make and maintain that investment. If the relation of viewing educational programs to science grades for girls is general, early viewing of PBS science shows might make an important contribution to girls' interest, motivation, success, and even career choice in science.

POLICY IMPLICATIONS

Because children appear to benefit from watching educational programming and may suffer from watching violent programming, it is important that educational programming be available for them to view and that parents be able to screen out programming that is potentially harmful. Our research provides support for two policies that have been specifically designed for these purposes.

One of the intents of the Children's Television Act of 1990 (and the more recent adoption of the FCC's processing guideline, known as the 3-hour rule) was to provide children with more educational programming on commercial broadcast stations. In order to gain expedited license renewal, commercial broadcast stations must air 3 hr of programming each week that is specifically designed to educate and inform children (FCC, 1996). So far, the policy does appear to be modestly successful at providing more educational television to children (Schmitt, 1999), although the majority of stations do not provide *more* than 3 hr each week. The possible longevity of educational effects of watching such programs at a young age makes policies such as this one even more important. In addition, it may be important to provide more diversity in educational and prosocial programming, because programs that teach in ways that go against normative developmental trends may be particularly effective.

The Telecommunications Act of 1996 offers parents a means of gaining greater control of the television content that comes into the home. First, many of the networks are voluntarily rating their television content, and second, "V-chip" technology is now available in new, U.S.-made television sets, so that parents can block the display of unwanted programming. Although the rating system of labeling programs for age-appropriateness and content is by no means perfect (e.g., Woodard, 1999), having content identifiers such as "FV" (for fantasy violence) may help parents to monitor their children's viewing. Our research suggests that children should view violent programming, such as cartoons, in moderation.

We hope that our results, which provide strong support for the potential of television to teach children, can be used to articulate a scientifically defensible set of public policies about what is good and not good for children in the media world.

A FINAL THOUGHT

Marshall McLuhan appears to have been wrong. The *medium* is not the message. The *message* is the message!

REFERENCES

Aitken, P. P., Eadie, D. R., Leathar, D. S., McNeill, R. E. J., & Scott, A. C. (1988). Television advertisements for drinks do reinforce under-age drinking. *British Journal of Addiction, 83,* 1399–1419.

Amabile, T. (1983). The social psychology of creativity: A componential conceptualization. *Journal of Personality and Social Psychology, 45,* 357–376.

Anderson, D. R., & Collins, P. A. (1988). *The impact on children's education: Television's influence on cognitive development* (Working Paper No. 2). Washington, DC: Office of Educational Research and Improvement.

Anderson, D. R., & Field, D. E. (1983). Children's attention to television: Implications for production. In M. Meyer (Ed.), *Children and the formal features of television*. Munchen, W. Germany: Saur.

Anderson, D. R., & Field, D. E. (1991). Online and offline assessment of the television audience. In J. Bryant & D. Zillmann (Eds.), *Responding to the screen: Reception and reaction processes* (pp. 199–216). Hillsdale, NJ: Erlbaum.

Anderson, D. R., Field, D. E., Collins, P. A., Lorch, E. P., & Nathan, J. G. (1985). Estimates of young children's time with television: A methodological comparison of parent reports with time-lapse video home observation. *Child Development, 56,* 1345–1357.

Anderson, D. R., Levin, S. R., & Lorch, E. P. (1977). The effects of TV program pacing on the behavior of preschool children. *AV Communication Review, 25,* 154–166.

Anderson, D. R., & Lorch, E. P. (1983). Looking at television: Action or reaction? In J. Bryant & D. R. Anderson (Eds.), *Children's understanding of television: Research on attention and comprehension*. New York: Academic.

Andison, F. S. (1977). TV violence and viewer aggression: A cumulation of study results 1956–1976. *Public Opinion Quarterly, 41,* 314–331.

Atkin, C. K., Hocking, J., & Block, M. (1984). Teenage drinking: Does advertising make a difference? *Journal of Communication, 28,* 71–80.

Ball, S. J., & Bogatz, G. A. (1970). *The first year of Sesame Street: An evaluation*. Princeton, NJ: Educational Testing Service.

Bandura, A. (1977). *Social learning theory* . Englewood Cliffs, NJ: Prentice-Hall.

Bandura, A. (1994). Social cognitive theory of mass communication. In J. Bryant & D. Zillmann (Eds.), *Media effects: Advances in theory and research*. Hillsdale, NJ: Erlbaum.

Barnett, W. S. (1995). Long-term effects of early childhood programs on cognitive and school outcomes. *The Future of Children, 5,* 25–50.

Baron, R., & Kenny, D. (1986). The moderator-mediator variable distinction in social psychological research: Conceptual, strategic, and statistical considerations. *Journal of Personality and Social Psychology, 56,* 596–607.

Bates, J. E., Pettit, G. S., & Dodge, K. A. (1995). Family and child factors in stability and change in children's aggressiveness in elementary school. In J. McCord (Ed.), *Coercion and punishment in long-term perspectives.* New York: Cambridge University Press.

Bechtel, R. B., Achelpohl, C., & Akers, R. (1972). Correlates between observed behavior and questionnaire responses on television viewing. In E. A. Rubinstein, G. A. Comstock, & J. P. Murray (Eds.), *Television and social behavior: Vol. 4. Television in day-to-day life: Patterns of use.* Washington, DC: U.S. Government Printing Office.

Beentjes, J. (1989). Learning from television and books: A Dutch replication study based on Salomon's model. *Educational Communication and Technology Journal, 37,* 47–58.

Bogatz, G. A., & Ball, S. J. (1972). *The impact of "Sesame Street" on children's first school experiences.* Princeton, NJ: Educational Testing Service.

Botta, R. A. (1999). Television images and adolescent girls' body image disturbance. *Journal of Communication, 49*(2), 22–41.

Breed, W., & DeFoe, J. R. (1983). Cigarette smoking on television: 1950–1982. *New England Journal of Medicine, 309,* 617

Brown, J. D., & Walsh-Childers, K. (1994). Effects of media on personal and public health. In J. Bryant & D. Zillmann (Eds.), *Media effects: Advances in theory and research.* Hillsdale, NJ: Erlbaum.

Bryant, J., Alexander, A., & Brown, D. (1983). Learning from educational television programs. In M. J. Howe (Ed.), *Learning from television: Psychological and educational research.* London: Academic.

Bryant, J., & Williams, M. (1997, April). *Impact of* Allegra's Window *and* Gullah Gullah Island *on preschool children's flexible thinking.* Paper presented at the biennial meeting of the Society for Research in Child Development, Washington, DC.

Burton, S., Calonico, J., & McSeveney, D. (1979). Growing up with television: Effects of preschool television watching on first-grade children. *Journal of Communication, 29,* 164–170.

Buss, A. H., & Durkee, A. (1957). An inventory of assessing different kinds of hostility. *Journal of Consulting Psychology, 21,* 343–349.

Calvert, S. L., & Huston, A. C. (1987). Television and children's gender schemata. In L. Liben & M. Signoriella (Eds.), *Children's gender schemata: Origins and implications.* San Francisco: Jossey-Bass.

Campbell, W. J. (1962). *Television and the Australian adolescent.* Sydney, Australia: Angus and Robertson.

Carpenter, C. J., Huston, A. C., & Spera, L. (1989). Children's use of time in their everyday activities during middle childhood. In M. Bloch & A. Pellegrini (Eds.), *The ecological context of children's play.* Norwood, NJ: Ablex.

Caucus for Producers, Writers, and Directors. (1983). *We've done some thinking.* Santa Monica, CA: Television Academy of Arts and Sciences.

Center for Research on the Influences of Television on Children (CRITC). (1983). *CRITC program categorization system coding manual.* Lawrence: University of Kansas.

Center for Science in the Public Interest (1992). *Survey of advertising on children's TV.* Washington, DC: Center for Science in the Public Interest.

Childs, J. H. (1979). Television viewing, achievement, IQ and creativity. (Doctoral dissertation, Brigham Young University). *Dissertation Abstracts International, 39,* 6531A.

Chirco, A. P. (1990). *An examination of stepwise regression models of adolescent alcohol and marijuana use with special attention to the television exposure-teen drinking issue.* Unpublished doctoral dissertation, Syracuse University, Syracuse, NY.

Clark, C., & King, K. (1992, October). *Television and the preparation of the mind for learning: Critical questions on the effects of television on the developing brains of young children.* Conference presentation at Department of Health and Human Services: Administration for Children and Families, Washington, DC.

Collins, W. A., & Getz, S. K. (1976). Children's social responses following modeled reactions to provocation: Prosocial effects of a television drama. *Journal of Personality*, **44**, 488–500.

Comstock, G. (1991). *Television and the American child*. Orlando, FL: Academic.

Comstock, G. A., & Paik, H. J. (1991). *Television and the American child*. Orlando, FL: Academic.

Condry, J. C. (1989). *The psychology of television*. Hillsdale, NJ: Erlbaum.

Cook, T. D., Appleton, H., Conner, R. F., Shaffer, A., Tamkin, G., & Weber, S. J. (1975). *"Sesame Street" revisited: A study in evaluation research*. New York: Russell Sage.

Cook, T. D., Kendziersky, D. A., & Thomas, S. V. (1983). The implicit assumptions of television: An analysis of the 1982 NIMH Report on Television and Behavior. *Public Opinion Quarterly*, **47**, 161–201.

Corteen, R. S., & Williams, T. M. (1986). Television and reading skills. In T. M. Williams (Ed.), *The impact of television: A natural experiment in three communities*. Orlando, FL: Academic.

Dietz, W. H. (1993). Television, obesity, and eating disorders. *Adolescent Medicine*, **75**, 543–549.

Dietz, W. H., & Gortmaker, S. L. (1985). Do we fatten our children at the television set? Obesity and television viewing in children and adolescents. *Pediatrics*, **75**, 807–813.

Dorr, A. (1986). *Television and children: A special medium for a special audience*. Beverly Hills, CA: Sage.

Drewnowski, A., Kurth, C. L., & Krahn, D. D. (1995). Effects of body image on dieting, exercise, and anabolic steroid use in adolescent males. *International Journal of Eating Disorders*, **17**, 381–386.

Dubow, E. F., & Miller, L. S. (1996). Processes influencing the relation between television violence viewing and aggressive behavior. In *Tuning in to young viewers: Social science perspectives on television*. Newbury Park, CA: Sage.

Duck, J. M. (1990). Children's ideals: The role of real-life versus media figures. *Australian Journal of Psychology*, **42**, 19–29.

Duck, J. M. (1992). *Heroes and heroines, real and fantastic: Children's involvement with media figures*. Paper presented at the Second International Media Ecology Conference, Mainz, Germany, April.

Duncan, O. D. (1961). A socioeconomic index for all occupations. In A. J. Reiss (Ed.), *Occupations and social status*. Glencoe, IL: Free.

Dunn, L. M., & Dunn, L. M. (1981). *Peabody Picture Vocabulary Test*. Circle Pines, MN: American Guidance Services.

Eccles (Parsons), J. S. (1983). Expectancies, values, and academic behaviors. In J. T. Spence (Ed.), *Achievement and achievement motives: Psychological and sociological approaches*. San Francisco: W.H. Freeman.

Eccles, J. S., & Barber, B. L. (1999). Student council, volunteering, basketball, or marching band: What kind of extracurricular involvement matters? *Journal of Adolescent Research*, **14** (1), 10–43.

Eccles, J. S., Wigfield, A., & Schiefele, U. (1997). Motivation to succeed. In W. Damon (Series Ed.) & N. Eisenberg (Ed.), *Handbook of child psychology: Vol. 3. Social, emotional, and personality development* (5th ed., pp. 1017–1096). New York: Wiley.

Entwisle, D. R., Alexander, K. L., & Olson, L. S. (1997). *Children, schools, and inequality*. Boulder, CO: Westview.

Eron, L. D., Lefkowitz, M. M., Huesmann, L. R., & Walder, L. O. (1972). Does television violence cause aggression? *American Psychologist*, **27**, 253–263.

Fallon, A. (1990). Culture in the mirror: Sociocultural determinants of body image. In T. F. Cash & T. Pruzinsky (Eds.), *Body images: Development, deviance, and change.* New York: Guilford.

Federal Communications Commission (FCC). (1996). *Policies and rules concerning children's television programming: Revision of programming policies for television broadcast stations* (MM Docket No. 93–48).

Fernie, D. E. (1981). Ordinary and extraordinary people: Children's understanding of television and real life models. In H. Kelly & H. Gardner (Eds.), *Viewing children through television.* San Francisco: Jossey-Bass.

Fetler, M. (1984). Television viewing and school achievement. *Journal of Communication, 35,* 104–118.

Friedrich, L. K., & Stein, A. H. (1973). Aggressive and prosocial television programs and the natural behavior of preschool children. *Monographs of the Society for Research in Child Development, 38*(4, Serial No. 151), 1–64.

Friedrich-Cofer, L. K., Huston-Stein, A., Kipnis, D. M., Susman, E. J., & Clewett, A. S. (1979). Environmental enhancement of prosocial television content: Effects on interpersonal behavior, imaginative play, and self-regulation in a natural setting. *Developmental Psychology, 15*(6), 637–646.

Furu, T. (1971). *The function of television for children and adolescents.* Tokyo: Monumenta Nipponica, Sophia University.

Gaddy, G. D. (1986). Television's impact on high school achievement. *Public Opinion Quarterly, 50,* 340–359.

Gardner, H. E. (1982). *Art, mind, and brain: A cognitive approach to creativity.* New York: Basic.

Garrow, J. S., & Webster, J. (1985). Quetelet's index (W/H^2) as a measure of fatness. *International Journal of Obesity, 9,* 147–153.

Gerbner, G., Gross, L., Morgan, M., & Signorielli, N. (1994). Growing up with television: The cultivation perspective. In J. Bryant & D. Zillmann (Eds.), *Media effects: Advances in theory and research.* Hillsdale, NJ: Erlbaum.

Gerbner, G., Morgan, M., & Signorielli, N. (1982). Programming health portrayals: What viewers see, say, and do. In D. Pearl, L. Bouthilet, & J. Lazar (Eds.), *Television and behavior: Ten years of scientific progress and implications for the eighties.* Washington, DC: U.S. Government Printing Office.

Gibbons, J., Anderson, D. R., Smith, R., Field, D. E., & Fischer, C. (1986). Young children's recall and reconstruction of audio and audiovisual narratives. *Child Development, 57,* 1014–1023.

Goldberg, M. E., Gorn, G. J., & Gibson, W. (1978). TV messages for snack and breakfast foods: Do they influence children's preferences? *Journal of Consumer Research, 5,* 48–54.

Golombok, S., & Fivush, R. (1994). *Gender development.* New York: Cambridge University Press.

Gonzalez-Lavin, A., & Smolak, L. (1995, March). *Relationship between television and eating problems in middle school girls.* Paper presented at the meeting of the Society for Research in Child Development, Indianapolis, IN.

Gordon, R. A. (1990). *Anorexia and bulimia: Anatomy of a social epidemic.* Cambridge, MA: Basil Blackwell.

Gorn, G. J., & Goldberg, M. E. (1982). Behavioral evidence of the effects of televised food messages on children. *Journal of Consumer Research, 9,* 200–205.

Gortmaker, S. L., Salter, C. A., Walker, D. K., & Dietz, W. H. (1990). The impact of television viewing on mental aptitude and achievement: A longitudinal study. *Public Opinion Quarterly, 54,* 594–604.

Greenfield, P. M., & Beagles-Roos, J. (1988). Radio vs. television: Their cognitive impact on children of different socioeconomic and ethnic groups. *Journal of Communication,* **38**(2), 71–92.

Greenfield, P. M., Farrar, D., & Beagles-Roos, J. (1986). Is the medium the message? An experimental comparison of the effects of radio and television on imagination. *Journal of Applied Developmental Psychology,* **7**, 201–218.

Greenfield, P. M. (1984). *Mind and media: The effects of television, video games, and computers.* Cambridge, MA: Harvard University Press.

Greenfield, P. M. (1994). Video games as cultural artifacts. *Journal of Applied Developmental Psychology,* **15**(1), 1–12.

Grube, J. W. (1993). Alcohol portrayals and alcohol advertising on television. *Alcohol Health and Research World,* **17**, 61–66.

Grube, J. W., & Wallack, L. (1994). Television advertising and drinking knowledge, beliefs, and intentions among school children. *American Journal of Public Health,* **84**, 254–259.

Hamgarth, F., & Reus, G. (1991, May). *Pluralism on the screen: Children's broadcasting in Germany.* Paper presented at the Annual Meeting of the International Communication Association, Chicago, IL.

Harrison, K., & Cantor, J. (1997). The relationship between media consumption and eating disorders. *Journal of Communication,* **47**, 40–67.

Harrison, L. F., & Williams, T. M. (1986). Television and cognitive development. In T. M. Williams (Ed.), *The impact of television: A natural experiment in three communities.* Orlando, FL: Academic.

Harter, S. (1988). *Self-perception profile for adolescents.* Denver: University of Denver.

Hartmann, T. (1996). *Beyond ADD: Hunting for reasons in the past & present.* Grass Valley, CA: Underwood.

Hayes, D. S., & Birnbaum, D. W. (1980). Preschoolers' retention of televised events: Is a picture worth a thousand words? *Developmental Psychology,* **16**(5), 410–416.

Healy, J. M. (1990). *Endangered minds: Why our children don't think.* New York: Simon and Schuster.

Hearold, S. (1986). A synthesis of 1043 effects of television on social behavior. In G. Comstock (Ed.), *Public communication and behavior* (Vol. 1). Orlando, FL: Academic.

Himmelweit, H. T., Oppenheim, A. N., & Vince, P. (1958). *Television and the child.* London: Oxford.

Hoffner, C. (1996). Children's wishful identification and parasocial interaction with favorite television characters. *Journal of Broadcasting & Electronic Media,* **40**, 389–402.

Hollingshead, A. B. (1975). *Four Factor Index of Social Status.* New Haven, CT: Yale University, Department of Psychology.

Hornik, R. (1978). Television access and slowing of cognitive growth. *American Educational Research Journal,* **15**, 1–15.

Hornik, R. (1981). Out-of-school television and schooling: Hypotheses and methods. *Review of Educational Research,* **51**, 193–214.

Huesmann, L. R. (1986). Psychological processes promoting the relation between exposure to media violence and aggressive behavior by the viewer. *Journal of Social Issues,* **42**(3), 125–140.

Huesmann, L. R., & Eron, L. D. (Eds.). (1986). *Television and the aggressive child: A cross-national comparison.* Hillsdale, NJ: Lawrence Erlbaum.

Huesmann, L. R., Eron, L. D., Lefkowitz, M. M., & Walder, L. O. (1984). The stability of aggression over time and generations. *Developmental Psychology,* **20**, 746–755.

Huesmann, L. R., & Miller, L. S. (1994). Long-term effects of repeated exposure to media violence in childhood. In L. R. Huesmann (Ed.), *Aggressive behavior: Current perspectives*. New York: Plenum.

Huston, A. C. (1983). Sex typing. In P. H. Mussen (Series Ed.) & E. M. Hetherington (Ed.), *Socialization, personality, and social development: Vol. 4. Handbook of child psychology* (4th ed.). New York: Wiley.

Huston, A. C., & Wright, J. C. (1983). Children's processing of television: The informative functions of formal features. In J. Bryant & D. R. Anderson (Eds.), *Children's understanding of television: Research on attention and comprehension*. New York: Academic.

Huston, A. C., & Wright, J. C. (1989). The forms of television and the child viewer. In G. Comstock & G. A. Comstock (Eds.), *Public communication and behavior* (Vol. 2). New York: Academic.

Huston, A. C., & Wright, J. C. (1994). Educating children with television: The forms of the medium. In D. Zillmann, J. Bryant, & A. C. Huston (Eds.), *Media, family, and children: Social scientific, psychodynamic, and clinical perspectives*. Hillsdale, NJ: Erlbaum.

Huston, A. C., & Wright, J. C. (1997). Mass media and children's development. In W. Damon (Series Ed.) and I. Sigel & K. A. Renninger (Eds.), *Child psychology in practice: Handbook of child psychology* (5th ed.). New York: Wiley.

Huston, A. C., Wright, J. C., Marquis, J., & Green, S. B. (1999). How young children spend their time: Television and other activities. *Developmental Psychology, 35,* 912–925.

Huston, A. C., Wright, J. C., Rice, M. L., Kerkman, D., & St. Peters, M. (1990). The development of television viewing patterns in early childhood: A longitudinal investigation. *Developmental Psychology, 26,* 409–420.

Huston, A. C., Wright, J. C., Wartella, E., Rice, M. L., Watkins, B. A., Campbell, T., & Potts, R. (1981). Communicating more than content: Formal features of children's television programs. *Journal of Communication, 31*(3), 32–48.

Jonsson, A. (1986). A threat or complement to school? *Journal of Educational Television, 12,* 29–38.

Joy, L. A., Kimball, M. M., & Zabrock, M. L. (1986). Television and children's aggressive behavior. In T. M. Williams (Ed.), *The impact of television: A natural experiment in three communities*. Orlando, FL: Academic.

Kaufman, L. (1980). Prime time nutrition. *Journal of Communication, 30*(3), 37–46.

Keith, T. Z., Reimers, T. M., Fehrmann, P. G., Pottebaum, S. M., & Aubey, L. W. (1986). Parental involvement, homework, and TV time: Direct and indirect effects on high school achievement. *Journal of Educational Psychology, 78,* 373–380.

Kelly, J. T., Patten, S. E., & Johannes, A. (1982). Analysis of self-reported eating and related behaviors in an adolescent population. *Nutrition Research, 2,* 417–432.

Kerns, T. Y. (1981). Television: A bisensory bombardment that stifles children's creativity. *Phi Delta Kappan, 62,* 456–457.

Kilbourne, J. (1994). Still killing us softly: Advertising and the obsession with thinness. In P. Fallon, M. A. Katzman, & S. C. Wooley (Eds.), *Feminist perspectives on eating disorders*. San Francisco: Guilford.

Kokko, K., & Pulkkinen, L. (2000). Aggression in childhood and long-term unemployment in adulthood: A cycle of maladaptation and some protective factors. *Developmental Psychology, 36,* 463–472.

Koolstra, C., & Van der Voort, T. (1996). Longitudinal effects of television on children's leisure-time reading: A test of three explanatory models. *Human Communication Research, 23,* 4–35.

Koshal, R. K., Koshal, M. A., & Gupta, A. K. (1996). Academic achievement and television viewing by eighth graders: A quantitative analysis. *Applied Economics, 28,* 919–928.

Kunkel, D., & Gantz, W. (1991). *Television advertising and drinking knowledge, beliefs, and intentions among school children* (Report to the Children's Advertising Review Unit of the Council of Better Business Bureaus). Bloomington: University of Indiana.

Lagerspetz, K., & Viemero, V. (1986). Television and aggressive behavior among Finnish children. In L. R. Huesmann & L. D. Eron (Eds.), *Television and the aggressive child: A cross-national comparison.* Hillsdale, NJ: Erlbaum.

Larson, R., Kubey, R. W., & Colletti, J. (1989). Changing channels: Early adolescent media choices and shifting investments in family and friends. *Journal of Youth & Adolescence,* **18,** 583–599.

Larson, R. W., & Verma, S. (1998). How children and adolescents spend time across the world: Work, play, and developmental opportunities. *Psychological Bulletin,* **125,** 701–736.

Lesser, G. S. (1972). Learning, teaching, and television production for children: The experience from "Sesame Street". *Harvard Educational Review,* **42,** 232–272.

Levine, M. P., & Smolak, L. (1996). Media as a context for the development of disordered eating. In L. Smolak & M. P. Levine (Eds.), *The developmental psychopathology of eating disorders: Implications for research, prevention, and treatment.* Mahwah, NJ: Erlbaum.

Liebert, R. M., & Sprafkin, J. (1988). *The early window: Effects of television on children and youth.* New York: Pergamon.

MacBeth, T. M. (1996). Indirect effects of television: Creativity, persistence, school achievement, and participation in other activities. In T. M. MacBeth (Ed.), *Tuning in to young viewers: Social science perspectives on television.* Thousand Oaks, CA: Sage.

Maccoby, E. E., & Jacklin, C. N. (1974). *The psychology of sex differences.* Stanford, CA: Stanford University Press.

Mahoney, J. L., & Cairns, R. B. (1997). Do extracurricular activities protect against early school dropout? *Developmental Psychology, 33*(2), 241–253.

Mander, G. (1978). *Four arguments for the elimination of television.* New York: William Morrow.

Medrich, E. A., Roizen, J. A., Rubin, V., & Buckley, S. (1982). *The serious business of growing up: A study of children's lives outside school.* Berkeley and Los Angeles: University of California Press.

Meline, C. W. (1976). Does the medium matter? *Journal of Communication, 26*(3), 81–89.

Mendelson, M. J., Mendelson, B. K., & Andrews, J. (2000). Self-esteem, body esteem, and body-mass in late adolescence: Is a competence × importance model needed? *Journal of Applied Developmental Psychology,* **21,** 249–266.

Mifflin, L. (1999, August 4). Pediatrics group offers tough rules for television. *New York Times.*

Milavsky, J. R., Stipp, H. H., Kessler, R. C., & Rubens, W. S. (1982). *Television and aggression: A panel study.* New York: Academic Press.

Milgram, R. M., Milgram, N. A., Rosenbloom, G., & Rabkin, L. (1978). Quantity and quality of creative thinking in children and adolescents. *Child Development,* **49,** 385–388.

Moody, K. (1980). *Growing up on television: The TV effect.* New York: Times.

Moore, D. C. (1990). Body image and eating behavior in adolescent boys. *American Journal of Diseases of Children,* **144,** 475–479.

Morgan, M., & Gross, L. (1982). Television and educational achievement and aspiration. In D. Pearl, L. Bouthilet, & J. Lazar (Eds.), *Television and behavior: Ten years of scientific progress and implications for the eighties: Vol. 2. Technical reports.* Washington, DC: Department of Health and Human Services.

Mumford, M. D., & Gustafson, S. (1988). Creativity syndrome. *Psychological Bulletin,* **103,** 27–43.

Murray, J. P., & Kippax, S. (1978). Children's social behavior in three towns with differing television experience. *Journal of Communication, 28*(1), 19–29.

Mutz, D. C., Roberts, D. F., & Van Vuuren, D. P. (1993). Reconsidering the displacement hypothesis: Television's influence on children's time use. *Communication Research,* **20,** 51–75.

Nakeo, K., & Treas, J. (1990). *Computing 1989 occupational prestige scores* (Methodological Report. General Social Survey, 70). Irvine: University of California, Department of Sociology.

National Science Foundation. (1977). *Research on the effects of television advertising on children: A review of the literature and recommendations for future research.* Washington, DC: Author.

Neapolitan, D. M., & Huston, A. C. (1994). *Educational content of children's programs on public and commercial television.* Lawrence, KS: Center for Research on the Influences of Television on Children.

Neuman, S. B. (1991). *Literacy in the television age: The myth of the TV effect.* Norwood, NJ: Ablex.

Neuman, S. B. (1995). *Literacy in the television age: The myth of the TV effect* (2nd ed.). Norwood, NJ: Ablex.

Paik, H., & Comstock, G. (1994). The effects of television violence on antisocial behavior: A meta-analysis. *Communication Research,* **21,** 516–546.

Pearl, D., Bouthilet, L., & Lazar, J. (Eds.). (1982). *Television and behavior: Ten years of scientific progress and implications for the eighties.* Washington, DC: U.S. Government Printing Office.

Peterson, C. C., Peterson, J. L., & Caroll, J. (1987). Television viewing and imaginative problem solving during preadolescence. *Journal of Genetic Psychology,* **147,** 61–67.

Pettit, G. S., Laird, R. D., Bates, J. E., & Dodge, K. A. (1997). Patterns of after-school care in middle childhood: Risk factors and developmental outcomes. *Merrill-Palmer Quarterly,* **43**(3), 515–538.

Pipher, M. (1994). *Reviving Ophelia: Saving the selves of adolescent girls.* New York: G.P. Putnam's Sons.

Posner, J. K., & Vandell, D. L. (1999). After-school activities and the development of low-income urban children: A longitudinal study. *Developmental Psychology,* **35,** 868–879.

Potter, W. J. (1987). Does television viewing hinder academic achievement among adolescents? *Human Communication Research,* **14,** 27–46.

Potter, W. J. (1986). Perceived reality and the cultivation hypothesis. *Journal of Broadcasting & Electronic Media,* **30,** 159–174.

Rice, M. L., Huston, A. C., Truglio, R., & Wright, J. C. (1990). Words from *Sesame Street:* Learning vocabulary while viewing. *Developmental Psychology,* **26,** 421–428.

Rice, M. L., & Woodsmall, L. (1988). Lessons from television: Children's word learning when viewing. *Child Development,* **59,** 420–429.

Richards, J. (1992). *Characteristics of students in high schools for the visual and performing arts.* (ERIC Document Reproduction Service No. ED 368 630)

Ritchie, D., Price, V., & Roberts, D. F. (1987). Television, reading, and reading achievement. *Communication Research,* **14,** 292–315.

RMC Research Corporation. (1989). *The impact of* Reading Rainbow *on libraries.* Hampton, NH: Author.

Roberts, D., Bachen, C., Hornby, M., & Hernandez-Ramos, P. (1984). Reading and television: Predictors of reading at different age levels. *Communication Research,* **11,** 9–50.

Robinson, T. N., Chen, H. L., & Killen, J. D. (1998). Television and music video exposure and risk of adolescent alcohol use. *Pediatrics,* **102,** 54–61.

Robinson, T. N., Hammer, L. D., Killen, J. D., Kraemer, H. C., Wilson, D. M., Hayward, C., & Taylor, C. B. (1993). Does television viewing increase obesity among adolescent girls? *Pediatrics,* **91,** 273–280.

Rosengren, K. E. (1994). Models of change and stability in adolescents' media use. In K. E. Rosengren (Ed.), *Media effects and beyond: Culture, socialization and lifestyles*. New York: Routledge.

Rosengren, K. E., Johnsson-Smaragdi, U., & Sonesson, I. (1994). For better and for worse: Effects studies and beyond. In K. E. Rosengren (Ed.), *Media effects and beyond: Culture, socialization and lifestyle*. New York: Routledge.

Rosengren, K. E., Wenner, L. A., & Palmgreen, P. (Eds.). (1985). *Media gratification research: Current perspectives*. Sage.

Rosengren, K. E., & Windahl, S. (1989). *Media matter: TV use in childhood and adolescence*. Norwood, NJ: Ablex.

Rothschild, M., Thorsen, E., Reeves, B., Hirsch, J., & Goldstein, R. (1986). EEG activity and the processing of television commercials. *Communication Research, 13*, 182–220.

Runco, M. A. (1991). *Divergent thinking*. Norwood, NJ: Ablex.

Runco, M. A., & Pezdek, K. (1984). The effect of television and radio on children's creativity. *Human Communication Research, 11*, 109–120.

Salomon, G. (1984). Television is "easy" and print is "tough": The differential investment of mental effort in learning as a function of perceptions and attributions. *Journal of Educational Psychology, 76*, 647–658.

Scarr, S., & McCartney, K. (1983). How people make their own environments: A theory of genotype → environment effects. *Child Development, 54*, 424–435.

Schmitt, K. L. (1999). *The three-hour rule: Is it living up to expectations?* (Report No. 30). Philadelphia: University of Pennsylvania, Annenberg Public Policy Center.

Schramm, W., Lyle, J., & Parker, E. B. (1961). *Television in the lives of our children*. Stanford, CA: Stanford University Press.

Signorielli, N. (1993). Television, the portrayal of women, and children's attitudes. In G. L. Berry & J. K. Asamen (Eds.), *Children and television: Images in a changing sociocultural world*. Newbury Park, CA: Sage.

Signorielli, N., & Morgan, M. (Eds.). (1990). *Cultivation analysis: New directions in media effects research*. Newbury Park, CA: Sage.

Silverstein, B., Peterson, B., & Perdue, L. (1986). Some correlates of the thin standard of bodily attractiveness for women. *International Journal of Eating Disorders, 5*, 895–905.

Singer, D., & Singer, J. L. (1990). *The house of make-believe: Play and the developing imagination*. Cambridge, MA: Harvard University Press.

Singer, J. L. (1980). The power and limits of television: A cognitive-affective analysis. In P. Tannenbaum (Ed.), *The entertainment function of television*. Hillsdale, NJ: Erlbaum.

Singer, J. L., & Singer, D. G. (1979). Come back, Mister Rogers, come back. *Psychology Today*, 56–60.

Singer, J. L., & Singer, D. G. (1981). *Television, imagination and aggression: A study of preschoolers*. Hillsdale, NJ: Erlbaum.

Singer, J. L., Singer, D., & Rapaczynski, W. (1984). Children's imagination as predicted by family patterns and television viewing: A longitudinal study. *Genetic Psychology Monographs, 110*, 43–69.

Stein, A. H., & Friedrich, L. K. (1975). The impact of television on children and youth. In E. M. Hetherington (Ed.), *Review of child development research* (Vol. 5). Chicago: University of Chicago Press.

Stern, M. (1973). Television and creativity: The effect of viewing certain categories of commercial television broadcasting on divergent thinking abilities of intellectually gifted elementary students. (Doctoral dissertation, 1973) *Dissertation Abstracts International, 34*, 3716A. (University Microfilms No. 73–31, 675).

Sternberg, R., & Lubart, T. (1991). An investment theory of creativity and its development. *Human Development, 34*, 1–31.

Stice, E., Schupak-Neuberg, E., Shaw, H. E., & Stein, R. I. (1994). Relation of media exposure to eating disorder symptomatology: An examination of mediating mechanisms. *Journal of Abnormal Psychology*, **103**, 836–840.

Strasburger, V. C. (1989). Why just say no won't work. *Journal of Pediatrics*, **114**, 676–681.

Strasburger, V. C. (1995). *Adolescents and the media: Medical and psychological impact.* Thousand Oaks, CA: Sage.

Taras, H. L., Sallis, J. F., Patterson, T. L., Nader, P. R., & Nelson, J. A. (1989). Television's influence on children's diet and physical activity. *Developmental and Behavioral Pediatrics*, **10**, 176–180.

Thompson, J. K., & Heinberg, L. J. (1993). Preliminary test of two hypotheses of body image disturbances. *International Journal of Eating Disorders*, **14**, 59–63.

Tiggemann, M., & Pickering, A. S. (1996). Role of television in adolescent women's body dissatisfaction and drive for thinness. *International Journal of Eating Disorders*, **20**, 199–203.

Timmer, S. G., Eccles, J. S., & O'Brien, K. (1985). How children use time. In F. T. Juster & F. P. Stafford (Eds.), *Time, goods, and well-being.* Ann Arbor: University of Michigan, Institute for Social Research.

Tower, R. B., Singer, D. G., Singer, J. L., & Biggs, A. (1979). Differential effects of television programming on preschoolers' cognition, imagination, and social play. *American Journal of Orthopsychiatry*, **49**, 265–281.

Truglio, R. T., Murphy, K. C., Oppenheimer, S., Huston, A. C., & Wright, J. C. (1996). Predictors of children's entertainment television viewing: Why are they tuning in? *Journal of Applied Developmental Psychology*, **17**, 474–494.

Tucker, L. A. (1982). Relationship between perceived somatotype and body cathexis of college males. *Psychological Reports*, **50**, 983–989.

Tucker, L. A. (1985). Television's role regarding alcohol use among teenagers. *Adolescence*, **20**, 593–598.

Valkenburg, P. M., & Beentjes, J. W. J. (1997). Children's creative imagination in response to radio and television stories. *Journal of Communication*, **47**(2), 21–38.

Valkenburg, P. M., & van der Voort, T. H. A. (1994). Influence of TV on daydreaming and creative imagination: A review of research. *Psychological Bulletin*, **116**, 316–339.

Valkenburg, P. M., & van der Voort, T. H. A. (1995). The influence of television on children's daydreaming styles: A 1-year panel study. *Communication Research*, **22**, 267–287.

Vibbert, M. M., & Meringoff, L. K. (1981). *Children's production and application of story imagery: A cross-medium investigation* (Technical Report No. 23). Cambridge, MA: Harvard University, Project Zero.

Vogler, M. (1975). *The relationship between television viewing and the variables concentration, creativity, and knowledge.* Unpublished doctoral dissertation. University of Vienna, Vienna, Austria.

Wade, S. (1971). Adolescence, creativity and media. *American Behavioral Scientist*, **14**, 341–351.

Wiegerman, O., Kuttschreuter, M., & Baarda, B. (1992). A longitudinal study of the effects of television viewing on aggressive and prosocial behaviors. *British Journal of Social Psychology*, **31**, 147–164.

Williams, P. A., Haertel, E. H., Walberg, H. J., & Haertel, G. D. (1982). The impact of leisure-time television on school learning: A research synthesis. *American Educational Research Journal*, **19**, 19–50.

Williams, T. M. (1986). Background and overview. In T. M. Williams (Ed.), *The impact of television: A natural experiment in three communities.* New York: Academic.

Williams, T. M., & Handford, A. G. (1986). Television and other leisure activities. In T. M.

Williams (Ed.), *The impact of television: A natural experiment in three communities.* Orlando FL: Academic.

Winn, M. (1977). *The plug-in drug: Television, children, and the family.* New York: Viking.

Winn, M. (1987). *Unplugging the plug-in drug.* New York: Penguin.

Wood, W., Wong, F. Y., & Chachere, J. G. (1991). Effects of media violence on viewers' aggression in unconstrained social interaction. *Psychological Bulletin, 109,* 371–383.

Woodard, E. H. (1999). *The 1999 state of children's television report: Programming for children over broadcast and cable television* (Report No. 28). Philadelphia: University of Pennsylvania, Annenberg Public Policy Center.

Wright, J. C., & Huston, A. C. (1983). A matter of form: Potentials of television for young viewers. *American Psychologist, 38,* 835–843.

Wright, J. C., & Huston, A. C. (1995). *Effects of educational TV viewing of lower income preschoolers on academic skills, school readiness, and school adjustment one to three years later.* Lawrence, KS: Center for Research on the Influences of Television on Children.

Zill, N., Davies, E., & Daly, M. (1994). *Viewing of Sesame Street by preschool children in the United States and its relation to school readiness.* Rockville, MD: Westat.

ACKNOWLEDGMENTS

The primary responsibilities of each of the authors were as follows: Daniel Anderson drafted Chapter 4, Achievement, and Chapter 9, Health-Related Behavior. Aletha Huston drafted Chapter 2, Method, Chapter 3, Teen Media Use, parts of Chapter 4 on achievement motivation, and Chapter 7, Aggression. Kelly Schmitt drafted Chapter 5, Creativity, and Chapter 6, Extracurricular Activities, and assisted with analyses in the early stages of Chapter 8, Health, Chapter 4, Achievement, and Chapter 3, Teen Media Use. Deborah Linebarger drafted Chapter 9, Self-Image, and assisted with analyses for Chapter 7, Aggression, Chapter 4, Achievement, and Chapter 3, Teen Media Use. John Wright drafted Chapter 1, Introduction, and was responsible for continuity and consistency in the editing of all chapters. He also drafted the abstract and coordinated the revisions of the manuscript, especially Chapter 10. All the authors participated in drafting the conclusion (Chapter 10), and all were involved in data collection, subject finding, data analyses, strategic decision making, and referencing.

Other individuals contributed major effort to this project. Patricia Collins supervised data cleaning and database management and many of the initial analyses reported in Chapter 2. She also contributed major effort on the initial analyses of academic achievement in Chapter 4. Ron Kessler provided advice about survey design and analysis. Betsy McElroy designed the basic recontact and case-finding procedures and supervised the telephone interviews, payments to subjects, and record keeping. She also helped develop the measures of self-image used in Chapter 10. Hari-haren Swami-Nathan supplied statistical advice, as did Sam Green. Carrie Lamble at the University of Kansas and Jill Sandidge at the University of Texas provided clerical and office management assistance. The idea of recontacting the children from the original studies emerged from discussions with Keith Mielke of Children's Television Workshop.

Many colleagues, research assistants, and former graduate students (in the early 1980s) played major roles in the design of the preschool projects and the collection of the initial data. Their contributions are acknowledged in the original publications of those studies (Huston, Wright, Rice, Kerkman, & St. Peters, 1990; Anderson, Field, Collins, Lorch, & Nathan, 1985).

Initial research at the University of Massachusetts and at the University of Kansas (CRITC) was supported by separate grants to both universities from the Spencer Foundation and by separate grants from the National Institute of Mental Health. Support for the recontact phase at both sites was provided by separate grants from the Markle Foundation, then directed by Lloyd Morrisett, who contributed wise advice to the study.

The work was conducted at five institutions whose administrative support was crucial to the project: Wright and Huston's Center for Research on the Influences of Television on Children (CRITC) at the University of Kansas, which moved with them to the University of Texas, Austin, was a loyal home to the Kansas contingent. Linebarger was a graduate student at the University of Kansas with Huston and Wright and moved with them to the University of Texas, Austin, where she completed a Ph.D. The Department of Psychology at the University of Massachusetts at Amherst was the home department for Anderson, who supervised the PhD work of Schmitt. The Juniper Gardens Children's Project in Kansas City, Kansas, provided a postdoctoral home for Linebarger, and the University of Pennsylvania's Annenberg Public Policy Center did the same for Schmitt.

Jill Sandidge provided invaluable administrative and support services throughout the preparation, revision, and completion of the manuscript.

All the authors thank their immediate and extended families, for love, support, and patience over many years.

Correspondence concerning this *Monograph* should be addressed to John C. Wright, Department of Human Ecology, GEA 117/A2700, University of Texas, Austin, TX 78712-1097 [e-mail: jwright@mail.utexas.edu].

COMMENTARY

CHILDREN AND ADOLESCENTS IN A CHANGING MEDIA WORLD

Reed Larson

This impressive study—the first to test the long-term influence of early childhood television viewing—arrives at a time when the media world of young people is rapidly changing. In the early 1980s, when the children in this study were exposed to television in ways that significantly impacted their development, there were three major networks, plus the Public Broadcasting System (PBS). Cable now brings dozens and progressively hundreds of channels into our homes, VCRs and electronic games provide innumerable additional content choices, and the rapidly expanding Internet portends a new world with unlimited attractive, easily available, and niche-targeted alternatives. In fact the computer has already replaced the television as the most liked medium of older children and adolescents (Roberts, Foehr, Rideout, & Brodie, 1999). In a prescient newspaper cartoon, a father asks his son what he knows about the dot.com ads he sees on television and is met with the response, "What's TV, Dad?" Science attempts to capture timeless truths, but, in the social sciences, historical change conspires to make research findings out of date. Could this study be antiquated even before it reaches your hands?

My answer to this question is a resounding "no": Don't discard this issue of your *SRCD Monographs*! The major finding of this research, in rebuttal to McLuhan, is that the medium is *not* the message. Rather, the authors have discovered that it is the *content* of the television shows children watch that predicts adolescent outcomes 11–13 years later. Contrary to warnings that the fast-paced images of *Sesame Street* and the recumbent passivity of viewers would be more influential than the educational content, this research indicates that content counts: Frequent childhood viewers of educational television had *higher* academic motivation and achievement in adolescence and showed evidence of *more*, not less, creativity and imagination. These relationships were robust with controls for (some though not all) possible confounding variables. These important findings rank with the groundbreaking studies demonstrating the long-term effectiveness of Head Start. Educational television works: It has sustained, long-term, positive relationships to development and behavior. In addition, this study extends a very well developed body of research demonstrating predictive relationships between children's watching violent television shows and subsequent aggressive behavior (Bushman & Huesmann, 2001; Strasburger, 1995). In this study, early childhood identification with television and its characters *combined with* viewing of violent programs was modestly associated with self-reported aggressive dispositions over a decade later.

If it is content that counts, these basic findings should hold for the future whether children are exposed to content through cable, a computer game, or over the Internet: Educational content leads to positive outcomes; antisocial content leads to antisocial outcomes. The findings confirm theories that children absorb the life world of information, images, emotions, norms, and values to which they are exposed through media (e.g., Bandura, 1994; Gerbner, Gross, Morgan, & Signorielli, 1994). Some media scholars would point out that the epistemology of longitudinal quantitative analysis, with its language of prediction, dependent variables, causal paths, and effects, gives short shrift to ways in which media viewers are participants in their own development. Children and adolescents actively choose media and actively assimilate its messages into their own meaning systems (J. Brown & Cantor, 2000). Gerbner et al. (1994) also point out that longitudinal studies focusing on individual differences, as this one does, do not provide information on shared and higher order societal effects. Hence the current research does not tell us about the *shared influence that television has had on all children,* including effects on society as a whole and on children's and adolescents' common symbolic culture. These points, however, do not detract from the fundamental finding that the positive versus negative content of television appears to be a significant factor in shaping and reinforcing the course of children's and adolescents' development.

I will go one step further and venture that the relevance of the study's findings are *magnified* for children of the present and future. Looking backward from 2015, we may see that this study was limited by a statistical "restricted range": that the constrained media choices available in the 1980s suppressed what, with more range, become stronger relationships. The extremes of positive and negative content available to children via media have been expanding since the early 1980s. Cable has brought more educational television options across more hours of the day. The future is likely to bring yet more, better, and more interactive educational media chioces. But likewise, the options for watching or interacting with violent content have increased (Subrahmanyam, Kraut, Greenfield, & Gross, 2001), and options for viewing sexual content and pornography via the Internet have greatly increased; indeed, many adolescents are being exposed to this sexual material (Donnerstein & Smith, 2001), sometimes involuntarily (Finkelhor, Mitchell, & Wolak, 2000). With more children and adolescents availing themselves of these extremes, one can expect the magnitude of positive and negative effects to increase.

Predicting the future, of course, is a fallible enterprise. A recent study group on "Adolescence in the 21st Century," organized by the Society for Research on Adolescence and the International Society for Behavioral Development, identified numerous directions of change that are likely to interact in complex and unpredictable ways (B. Brown, Larson, & Saraswathi, in press; Larson, Mortimer, & Brown, in press; Mortimer & Larson, in press). Nonetheless, I think several trends also point to the magnification of media effects. First, despite the cartoon I mentioned above, there is limited evidence thus far that television viewing is declining as a result of new media. Internet use appears to be added *on top of* use of other media. The total number of hours of the day that youth are exposed to media appears to be increasing (Roberts, 2000; Subrahmanyam et al., 2001), hence magnifying its impact. Second, parents' ability to regulate media use seems to be declining, especially for older children. Research finds that more parents than in the past report setting rules on television viewing but that they are not very effective (Hogan, 2001). More youth now have television sets, electronic games, and computers in their bedrooms, putting them further out of reach of parental monitoring (Jordan, 2001; Roberts, 2000). Third, there is reason to suspect that the new, more interactive media have greater impact on children than passive media like television. Current theories and research in education indicate that, compared to unidirectional "teaching," interactive learning is more effective (Eccles, Wigfield, & Schiefele, 1998): It leads to deeper and more effectual cognitive processing. Thus we can expect that the child who is passively watching Big Bird display words that start with *m* will learn less than the child who is directly interacting, who is actively thinking up and shouting out *m*-words, then getting immediate feedback from the feathered friend. Similarly, it seems likely that the impact of simply watching characters being killed on television will be exceeded for a child playing a computer game who is doing the virtual killing. In sum, these trends point toward children's media use involving more choices, more contact time, and fewer controls and employing more effective methods.

The combined influence of these multiple trends is likely to be a widening divergence between the negative and positive developmental pathways articulated by these authors in their conclusion. On the one hand, research indicates that children with antisocial tendency receive less monitoring from parents (Patterson, DeBaryshe, & Ramsey, 1989) and are most likely to choose violent media content (Cantor, 2000; Roe, 1995). Thus, this group is likely to enter a "spiral" in which aggressive content is chosen and an aggressive worldview is reinforced. In contrast, another set of children have parents who monitor their television use, choose to view more educational media content, and are reinforced for learning. With more diverse and more effective media choices, the "reciprocal determinism" of media choice and media effects for both groups of youth are likely to be accentuated.

This brings us to the question of what can be done to narrow the divergence between these developmental paths—or rather to minimize the number of youth entering the negative spiral, and maximize those entering the positive one? In a free society there are constraints on direct top-down intervention. The Internet, in particular, has been developed with an ethos that is opposed to government controls (Hellenga, in press), and its internationalization makes that task even harder. Within these constraints, one focus of policy must be ensuring that there is a rich menu of high-quality, age-appropriate educational media venues for children and adolescents to choose amongst. As these authors point out, on a per child basis, educational television is a comparatively inexpensive intervention. A priority should be preserving and expanding this—now proven—means of positively affecting youth. The authors recommend policy initiatives to increase the quantity and quality of educational television on the major networks. Looking ahead, it seems essential to establish a defined territory of well-crafted educational content on the Internet (perhaps with its own dot.suffix). We face a future in which commercial interests sponsor enticing Internet playrooms, containing numerous simultaneous interactive and more traditional, television-like choices. There need to be similar Internet "safe zones" or developmentally facilitative sites (Montgomery, 2001) that provide rich menus of PBS-equivalent fare to all homes at all hours of the day.

Of course, making educational content available, even that of high quality, does not mean it will be viewed. The ability of policy to influence children's media choices appears to depend largely on influencing parents' exercise of control. Missing from this valuable study is attention to the ways in which parents shape children's media choices and experience. Although there is much discussion about the important role parents play as monitors and interpreters of television (Hogan, 2001), there is a crucial need for research that understands and critically evaluates this role. Part of the reason parents are often ineffectual may be because, in coviewing situations including households where the television is always on continuously, media choices are dictated by parents' entertainment preferences rather than the educational needs of children. It is next to impossible to impart a healthy media diet to children when parents' viewing is the equivalent of junk food.

This leads us to the other side of the policy equation, which is how to reduce children's exposure to unhealthy media diets. Whereas coviewing with parents, I think, is shaped by parents' entertainment preferences, the problem with solitary viewing, which increases in adolescence (Larson, Kubey, & Colletti, 1989), is that it is outside parents' field of vision. In homes with parents committed to monitoring, this should not be a big obstacle. I believe that had the V-chip been introduced along with television, it would have been more widely utilized by parents than it currently is. It seems imperative that, as with the introduction of seat belts, we try to gradually make up for the lost opportunity with television and not lose the chance to get in on the ground floor with new media. Software is now in widespread use that allows employers to monitor their employees' Internet use. It should be possible for similar software to be available to parents to monitor (and limit) their children's use of all new and old media, just as they monitor other activities in children's lives. The bottom line is that we need to be assertive and creative in influencing how families interact with these new media.

In closing, I would highlight the vital importance of further developmental research. Media policy and education needs to be based on a solid base of knowledge (J. Brown & Cantor, 2000), and, in my view, developmental science has given insufficient attention to this important arena of development. This landmark study and other research further establishes media as an important socializing influence, with long-term effects, but we really know comparatively little about it, and the knowledge we do have is outside the purview of most developmental scientists. Given that the number of hours of the day devoted to media generally exceeds that spent interacting with family members and with friends (Larson & Verma, 1999)—and is growing—we should consider giving it equivalent attention to these other well-studied developmental contexts in our textbooks, theories, and future research. More developmental studies, particularly longitudinal studies, are needed.

Building from this study, first, we should ask whether early childhood is a sensitive or critical period for media effects or whether the strength of relationships found here would be similar across developmental periods. Provocatively, the authors suggest that because young children have few preexisting scripts for social or conflict situations, media may be particularly influential at this period.

Second, as the authors recommend, research needs to reach beyond the largely White, working- to middle-class children studied here. Since lower socioeconomic status and minority youth tend to watch more hours of television (Larson & Verma, 1999), one might expect effects that are as strong or stronger for these groups. But we cannot assume this; variations in processes between and within different groups need to be examined. Given that other cultural groups have often been unfairly portrayed or simply not represented in the media, it is critical to understand how media experience interacts with the development of ethnic concepts and identity for both minority and majority youth (Berry, 2000).

Third, the current study leaves us guessing what happened between age 5 and late adolescence. Longitudinal research sometimes replaces the infamous black box with a mysterious "dark tunnel." We need to know about the intervening processes: how children make media choices; the influence of personality dispositions on media diets and impacts; the role of parents, siblings, and friends; and the paths of influence across adjacent developmental periods.

Fourth, in addition to the rich list of outcome variables examined here, more longitudinal research is needed to assess the effects of media's commercialism, and as children get older, its sexual content.

Lastly, I have predicted above that the influences of media on children will increase with the growth of new media and their increasing diversity and sophistication. But this is only a hypothesis, and there is undoubtedly far greater underlying complexity in the use and influence of these new media that needs to be charted. Developmental scholars need to quickly catch up and get on top of this important and changing context of children's and adolescents' experience.

Acknowledgment

The author's work on the commentary was partly supported by a grant from the William T. Grant Foundation on "Adolescence in the 21st Century."

References

Bandura, A. (1994). Social cognitive theory of mass communication. In J. Bryant & D. Zillman (Eds.), *Media effects: Advances in theory and research.* Hillsdale, NJ: Lawrence Erlbaum.

Berry, G. (2000). Multicultural media portrayals and the changing demographic landscape: The psychosocial impact of television representations on the adolescent of color. *Journal of Adolescent Health,* **27S,** 57–60.

Brown, B., Larson, R., & Saraswathi, T. S. (in press). *The world's youth: Adolescence in eight regions of the globe.* New York: Cambridge University Press.

Brown, J., & Cantor, J. (2000). An agenda for research on youth and the media. *Journal of Adolescent Health,* **27S,** 2–7.

Bushman, B., & Huesmann, L. R. (2001). Effects of televised violence on aggression. In D. Singer & J. Singer (Eds.), *Handbook of children and the media*. Thousand Oaks, CA: Sage.

Cantor, J. (2000). Media violence. *Journal of Adolescent Health*, **27S**, 30–34.

Donnerstein, E., & Smith, S. (2001). Sex in the media: Theory, influences, and solutions. In D. Singer & J. Singer (Eds.), *Handbook of children and the media*. Thousand Oaks, CA: Sage.

Eccles, J. S., Wigfield, A., & Schiefele, U. (1998). Motivation to succeed. In N. Eisenberg (Ed.), *Handbook of child psychology: Social, emotional, and personality development* (5th ed., Vol. 3). New York: John Wiley & Sons.

Finkelhor, D., Mitchell, K., & Wolak, J. (2000). Online victimization: A report on the nation's youth. Crimes Against Children Research Center, University of New Hampshire [On-line]. Available: http://www.missingkids.com

Gerbner, G., Gross, L., Morgan, M., & Signorielli, N. (1994). Growing up with television: The cultivation perspective. In J. Bryant & D. Zillmann (Eds.), *Media effects: Advances in theory and research*. Hillsdale, NJ: Lawrence Erlbaum.

Hellenga, K. (in press). Social space, the final frontier: Adolescents on the Internet. In J. Mortimer & R. Larson (Eds.), *The future of adolescent experience: Societal trends and the transition to adulthood*. New York: Cambridge University Press.

Hogan, M. (2001). Parents and other adults: Models and monitors of healthy media habits. In D. Singer & J. Singer (Eds.), *Handbook of children and the media*. Thousand Oaks, CA: Sage.

Jordan, A. (2001). Public policy and private practice: Government regulation and parental control of children's television use in the home. In D. Singer & J. Singer (Eds.), *Handbook of children and the media*. Thousand Oaks, CA: Sage.

Larson, R., Kubey, R., & Colletti, J. (1989). Changing channels: Early adolescent media choices and shifting investments in family and friends. *Journal of Youth and Adolescence*, **18**(5), 583–600.

Larson, R., Mortimer, J., & Brown, B. B. (Eds.). (in press). Adolescence in the 21st century [Special issue]. *Journal of Research on Adolescence*.

Larson, R., & Verma, S. (1999). How children and adolescents around the world spend time: Work, play, and developmental opportunities. *Psychological Bulletin*, **125**(6), 701–736.

Montgomery, K. (2001). Digital kids: The new on-line children's consumer culture. In D. Singer & J. Singer (Eds.), *Handbook of children and the media*. Thousand Oaks, CA: Sage.

Mortimer, J. & Larson, R. (in press). *The future of adolescent experience: Societal trends and the transition to adulthood*. New York: Cambridge University Press.

Patterson, G., DeBaryshe, B., & Ramsey, E. (1989). A developmental perspective on antisocial behavior. *American Psychologist*, **44**, 329–335.

Roberts, D. (2000). Media and youth: Access, exposure, and privatization. *Journal of Adolescent Health*, **27S**, 8–14.

Roberts, D. Foehr, U., Rideout, V., & Brodie, M. (1999). *Kids and media @ the new millennium*. Menlo Park, CA: Kaiser Family Foundation.

Roe, K. (1995). Adolescents' use of socially disvalued media: Toward a theory of media delinquency. *Journal of Youth and Adolescence*, **24**, 617–631.

Strasburger, V. C. (1995). *Adolescents and the media*. Thousand Oaks, CA: Sage.

Subrahmanyam, K., Kraut, R., Greenfield, P., & Gross, E. (2001). New forms of electronic media: The impact of interactive games and the Internet on cognition, socialization and behavior. In D. Singer & J. Singer (Eds.), *Handbook of children and the media*. Thousand Oaks, CA: Sage.

CONTRIBUTORS

Daniel R. Anderson (PhD, 1971, Brown University) is Professor of Psychology at the University of Massachusetts at Amherst. He has studied children's attention to and active processing of television, especially of educational television. He was first to observe and explain the phenomenon of attentional inertia, which serves as a counterbalance to habituation to maintain attention in certain contexts. He has served as a consultant to the producers of many PBS and commercial educational programs for children.

Aletha C. Huston (PhD, 1965, University of Minnesota) is the Priscilla Pond Flawn Regents Professor of Child Development at the University of Texas, Austin. She is the lead author of *Big World, Small Screen: The Role of Television in American Society* and the recipient of the Urie Bronfenbrenner Award from Division 7 of the American Psychological Association (1999). She was the editor of the 1991 book *Children in Poverty: Child Development and Public Policy*. A member of the MacArthur Network on development in middle childhood, she is an investigator in Project "New Hope," an experimental intervention with poor families in Milwaukee, and a member of the steering committee for the NICHD National Study of Child Care. She is Co-Director of CRITC.

Kelly L. Schmitt (PhD, 1997, University of Massachusetts) is a Research Fellow at the Annenberg Public Policy Center at the University of Pennsylvania. She has published numerous articles on children's television viewing and is co-authoring a book on the state of children's television that will explore the economic, regulatory, and social forces that shape what children see in the new media environment. She has also served as a consultant for Jim Henson Productions, Nickelodeon, and A.R.C. Consulting.

155

Deborah L. Linebarger (PhD, 1998, University of Texas at Austin) is an Assistant Research Professor at the Juniper Gardens Children's Project, an affiliate of the Schiefelbusch Institute for Life Span Studies at the University of Kansas. Her research interests include literacy, language, and other cognitive outcomes in the contexts of early television viewing and child care experiences, especially with children who come from impoverished backgrounds.

John C. Wright (PhD, 1960, Stanford University) is Senior Lecturer and Senior Research Scientist in the Departments of Human Ecology (Division of Human Development and Family Science) and Radio, Television, and Film at the University of Texas at Austin. He founded (with Aletha Huston) the Center for Research on the Influences of Television on Children (CRITC) at the University of Kansas, where he was Professor of Human Development and Family Life until 1996, when he, Huston, Linebarger, and CRITC all moved to The University of Texas.

Reed Larson is Professor of Human Development and Family Studies at the University of Illinois at Urbana-Champaign. His research focuses on adolescents' daily emotions and experience, especially in the context of families and after-school activities.

STATEMENT OF EDITORIAL POLICY

The *Monographs* series is devoted to publishing developmental research that generates authoritative new findings and uses these to foster fresh, better integrated, or more coherent perspectives on major developmental issues, problems, and controversies. The significance of the work in extending developmental theory and contributing definitive empirical information in support of a major conceptual advance is the most critical editorial consideration. Along with advancing knowledge on specialized topics, the series aims to enhance cross-fertilization among developmental disciplines and developmental subfields. Therefore, clarity of the links between the specific issues under study and questions relating to general developmental processes is important. These links, as well as the manuscript as a whole, must be as clear to the general reader as to the specialist. The selection of manuscripts for editorial consideration, and the shaping of manuscripts through reviews-and-revisions, are processes dedicated to actualizing these ideals as closely as possible.

Typically *Monographs* entail programmatic large-scale investigations; sets of programmatic interlocking studies; or—in some cases—smaller studies with highly definitive and theoretically significant empirical findings. Multi-authored sets of studies that center on the same underlying question can also be appropriate; a critical requirement here is that all studies address common issues, and that the contribution arising from the set as a whole be unique, substantial, and well integrated. The needs of integration preclude having individual chapters identified by individual authors. In general, irrespective of how it may be framed, any work that is judged to significantly extend developmental thinking will be taken under editorial consideration.

To be considered, submissions should meet the editorial goals of *Monographs* and should be no briefer than a minimum of 80 pages (including references and tables). There is an upper limit of 150–175 pages. Only in exceptional circumstances will this upper limit be modified (please submit four copies). Because a *Monograph* is inevitably lengthy and usually substantively complex, it is particularly important that the text be well organized and written in clear, precise, and literate English. Note, however, that authors from non-English-speaking countries should not be put off by this stricture. In accordance with the general aims of SRCD, this series is actively interested in promoting international exchange of developmental research. Neither membership in the Society nor affiliation with the academic discipline of psychology is relevant in considering a *Monographs* submission.

The corresponding author for any manuscript must, in the submission letter, warrant that all coauthors are in agreement with the content of the manuscript. The corresponding author also is responsible for informing all coauthors, in a timely manner, of manuscript submission, editorial decisions, reviews received, and any revisions recommended. Before publication, the corresponding author also must warrant in the submission letter that the study has been conducted according to the ethical guidelines of the Society for Research in Child Development.

Potential authors who may be unsure whether the manuscript they are planning would make an appropriate submission are invited to draft an outline of what they propose, and send it to the Editor for assessment. This mechanism, as well as a more detailed description of all editorial policies, evaluation processes, and format requirements, can be found at the Editorial Office web site (http://astro.temple.edu/~overton/monosrcd.html) or by contacting the Editor, Willis F. Overton, Temple University–Psychology, 1701 North 13th St.—Rm. 567, Philadelphia, PA 19122-6085 (e-mail: monosrcd@blue.vm.temple.edu) (telephone: 1-215-204-7718).

Monographs of the Society for Research in Child Development (ISSN 0037-976X), one of three publications of the Society for Research in Child Development, is published four times a year by Blackwell Publishers, Inc., with offices at 350 Main Street, Malden, MA 02148, USA, and 108 Cowley Road, Oxford OX4 1JF, UK. Call US 1-800-835-6770, fax: (781) 388-8232, or e-mail: subscrip@ blackwellpub.com. A subscription to *Monographs of the SRCD* comes with a subscription to *Child Development* (published six times a year in February, April, June, August, October, and December). A combined package rate is also available with the third SRCD publication, *Child Development Abstracts and Bibliography*, published three times a year.

INFORMATION FOR SUBSCRIBERS   For new orders, renewals, sample copy requests, claims, change of address, and all other subscription correspondence, please contact the Journals Subscription Department at the publisher's Malden office.

INSTITUTIONAL SUBSCRIPTION RATES FOR MONOGRAPHS OF THE SRCD/CHILD DEVELOPMENT 2001   The Americas $293, Rest of World £192. All orders must be paid by credit card, business check, or money order. Checks and money orders should be made payable to Blackwell Publishers. Canadian residents please add 7% GST.

INSTITUTIONAL SUBSCRIPTION RATES FOR MONOGRAPHS OF THE SRCD/CHILD DEVELOPMENT/CHILD DEVELOPMENT ABSTRACTS AND BIBLIOGRAPHY 2001   The Americas $369, Rest of World £246. All orders must be paid by credit card, business check, or money order. Checks and money orders should be made payable to Blackwell Publishers. Canadian residents please add 7% GST.

BACK ISSUES   Back issues are available from the publisher's Malden office.

MICROFORM   The journal is available on microfilm. For microfilm service, address inquiries to Bell and Howell Information and Learning, 300 North Zeeb Road, Ann Arbor, MI 48106-1346, USA. Bell and Howell Serials Customer Service Department: 1-800-521-0600 ×2873.

POSTMASTER   Periodicals postage paid at Boston, MA, and additional offices. Send all address corrections to Blackwell Publishers, Journals Subscriptions Department, 350 Main Street, Malden, MA 02148.

FORTHCOMING

Rhythms of Dialogue in Infancy: Coordinated Timing in Development—
*Joseph Jaffe, Beatrice Beebe, Stanley Feldstein, Cynthia L. Crown, and
Michael D. Jasnow* (SERIAL NO. 265, 2001)

CURRENT

Parameters of Remembering and Forgetting in the Transition from
Infancy to Early Childhood—*P. J. Bauer, J. A. Wenner,
P. L. Dropik, and S. S. Wewerka* (SERIAL NO. 263, 2000)

Breaking the Language Barrier: An Emergentist Coalition Model for
the Origins of Word Learning—*George J. Hollich, Kathy Hirsh-Pasek,
Roberta Michnick Golinkoff* (SERIAL NO. 262, 2000)

Across the Great Divide: Bridging the Gap Between Understanding of
Toddlers' and Other Children's Thinking—*Zhe Chen and Robert Siegler*
(SERIAL NO. 261, 2000)

Making the Most of Summer School: A Meta-Analytic and
Narrative Review—*Harris Cooper, Kelly Charlton, Jeff C. Valentine,
and Laura Muhlenbruck* (SERIAL NO. 260, 2000)

Adolescent Siblings in Stepfamilies: Family Functioning
and Adolescent Adjustment—*E. Mavis Hetherington,
Sandra H. Henderson, and David Reiss* (SERIAL NO. 259, 1999)

Atypical Attachment in Infancy and Early Childhood
Among Children at Developmental Risk—
Joan I. Vondra and Douglas Barnett (SERIAL NO. 258, 1999)

The Stories That Families Tell: Narrative Coherence, Narrative
Interaction, and Relationship Beliefs—*Barbara H. Fiese,
Arnold J. Sameroff, Harold D. Grotevant, Frederick S. Wamboldt,
Susan Dickstein, and Deborah Lewis Fravel* (SERIAL NO. 257, 1999)

Continuity and Change in the Social Competence of Children With
Autism, Down Syndrome, and Developmental Delays—
Marian Sigman and Ellen Ruskin (SERIAL NO. 256, 1999)

Social Cognition, Joint Attention, and Communicative Competence
from 9 to 15 Months of Age—*Malinda Carpenter, Katherine Nagell,
and Michael Tomasello* (SERIAL NO. 255, 1998)